School Exclusions
The Parent Guide

Abigail Hawkins

978 1091514201

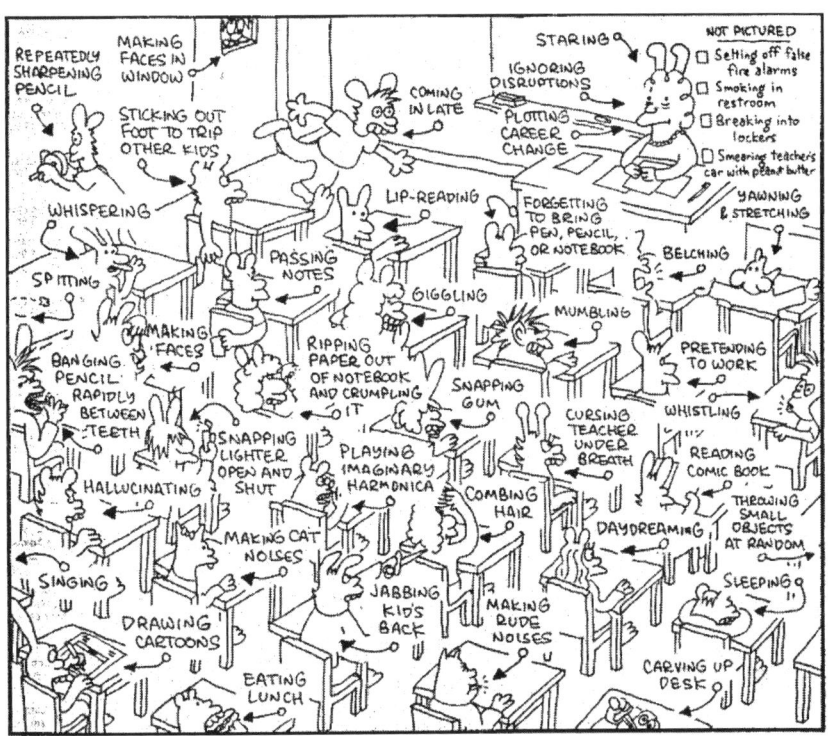

School Exclusion – The Parent Guide

Copyright © 2019 by Abigail Hawkins

All rights reserved. No part of this publication may be reproduced, distributed, or transmitted in any form or by any means, including photocopying, recording, or other electronic or mechanical methods, without the prior written permission of the publisher, except in the case of brief quotations embodied in critical reviews and certain other noncommercial uses permitted by copyright law. For permission requests, email to the author, addressed "Attention: Permissions Coordinator," at the address below.

All children's names and the schools in this book have been changed to protect the identity of individuals.

permission@sencosolutions.co.uk

www.sencosolutions.co.uk

Dedication:

To my husband, Gavin, and all of our boys who stayed out of my way whilst I tried to string, sensible, sentences together.

Contents

Contents 3
Preface 5
Introduction 7
   Acronyms and Eduspeak 9
   Context 11
Exclusions 19
   Behaviour Policies 21
   Who can exclude a child from school? 24
   What can a child be excluded for? 25
   Persistent Disruption 29
   They cannot be excluded for… 30
   It didn't happen in school… 34
   What are the different types of exclusion? 37
   Covert exclusions 39
   How long can an exclusion be for? 40
   Fixed Term Exclusions 41
   Fixed-Term pending Permanent Exclusions 42
   Permanent Exclusions 44
Alternatives 47
   Early Intervention 48
   Part-time Timetables 50
   Managed Moves 53
   Pupil Referral Unit 56
   Alternative Provision 58
   Internal 60
   Pastoral Support Plan 61
   Transfer 62
School Procedure 63
   The balance of proof 64
   Duty of care 66
   The letter 67
   An Education 68
   Dealing with the school roll 70
   School must tell 71
   Penalties and fines 72
   Reintegration 73
Incident procedure 75
   Pupil voice 77
   Statements 78

Letters	79
Parent Procedure	81
Subject Access Request (SAR)	82
Complaints	84
Challenging exclusion	86
Vulnerable Groups	87
SEN	91
Equalities Act & Discrimination	96
Governors	99
Who	100
What is an SEN Expert?	101
A letter to the governors	102
Appeals	105
Permanent Exclusions (15+days/Exams)	106
Fixed-Term Exclusions (6-14 days)	110
Fixed-Term Exclusion (up to 5 days)	112
Independent Review Panel (IRP)	113
Judicial Review	115
First Tier Tribunal	116
Parental responsibility	117
Not in school during an exclusion	118
Absence	119
Exams	121
Public spaces	122
The different perspectives	123
The national view & effectiveness of exclusion	123
The Student perspective	124
The Parent perspective	126
The School perspective	129
The future (for your child)	133
Me and Controversy	135
FAQ	137
HELP	145
Appendix	147
Sample Fixed-term exclusion letter	148
Sample Permanent exclusion letter	149
Governors uphold permanent exclusion letter	150
Law:	151
Exclusion from maintained schools, academies and pupil referral units in England	156
Bibliography	205
Index	207

Preface

I've worked in education for well over 20 years. There is little I haven't seen or dealt with in that time. As the SENCO in most of the establishments I've worked with it would be fair to

Exclusions are emotive

say I've dealt with more exclusions than the normal classroom teacher might come across in their career. Having never ascended the ranks to headteacher though, I am not guilty of having ever 'excluded' a pupil.

Exclusions are an emotive subject, and everyone has their viewpoint (me included). There is then the law and there are school rules. Sometimes, they all align with each other!

This is not a book for educators on how to avoid exclusions, there are many of these available – in fact it assumes an exclusion has taken place or is on the horizon. This book advises parents (and others) on the lawful situation and illustrates with real examples (names changed).

I am a firm believer that behaviour is a form of communication. Disruptive behaviour can also be a sign of an unmet need. That said SEN (special education needs) are not an excuse or passport for poor behaviour choices. All staff and students in a school have a right to feel safe in their environment. We all make mistakes and the child or young person needs to know that their actions and behaviours have consequences.

Do I have the right or the experience to talk to parents about exclusions? I'd like to think so. I'm Mum to 4 boys, all of whom bring their own challenges. None have ever strayed far enough to get a formal school exclusion, but one has been close! I thoroughly suspect the school didn't go through with it in the end as they knew I would be able to challenge their practice. Sat on the other side of the fence as a SENCO and now as a chair of governors within schools I think I know enough of the inside information to present all sides of the story in a fair and reasoned manner.

You will find I use the same names throughout the book for our excluded children, apologies to anyone who shares their names (and my maternal grandparents)!

Tom and Nell.

Introduction

Why are you reading this book?

Take a deep breath, grab a cup of tea (or something stronger) and watch TV for an hour/go for a run/bake a cake. The chances are if you are reading this book, your child has just been excluded from school and you want to know more! The most important thing is to not panic and take a little time for yourself to gather your thoughts. That way, whether it's a fair exclusion and you need to look at the future, or an unfair exclusion and you need to appeal, you will have the brain-space to generate a coherent argument when dealing with what happens next.

The last section of this book contains the statutory guidance from the DfE, feel free to jump to that section. However, knowing how these documents can be rather tricky to navigate I have used the first part of the book to try to explain this document and illustrate with examples. (Warning: I have a very dry sense of humour and I do use real, although anonymised, examples from 23 years of working in education.)

It is important to understand that the DfE guidance is for maintained schools, academies AND pupil referral units. I often see parents state that they have been told their school is an academy and they can do what they want…NO, they can't! It's the same guidance as for a maintained school with some slight differences in the appeals process and who is responsible for education.

The other thing I often hear is parents jumping straight to OFSTED, the local authority and their MP to complain. Sorry, it won't get you anywhere any faster. Every school has to have a complaints process and you have to follow it. It will be the first thing any of the above bodies ask, and should you have not done so, they simply forward your information to the school to pick up back at the beginning again.

An exclusion is inconvenient. It might involve changing family plans, having to take unpaid time off work and has repercussions beyond just your child. Whether or not you 'agree' with the exclusion, it is important that the day is not made 'special' for your child (sorry). Otherwise, there will be a perverse incentive to get excluded again to enjoy the fun you've had together!

I know, how horrid I sound saying that, and I deleted it many times when editing this book. I also know that when a parent really disagrees with an exclusion, they often try to make it up to their child with a special day together. I've seen many of those children come back in to school and escalate their behaviours in order to get excluded again.

I had one student who was excluded for spitting on a member of staff and verbally abusing them. The staff member had asked for his homework. The child was absent the day the homework had been set and the staff member should have realised, however the reaction of the student was unacceptable. The parent disagreed and felt it was OK for their child to respond the way they had, and it was the teacher's fault for asking. He received a 1.5-day exclusion.

On return, I asked him what he had done in his time off (I was hoping he would hand me his work). "We went straight from school to McDonalds, then we went to the cinema. When we got home, we had Chinese takeaway. Yesterday, Dad came over and took me to Alton Towers, it was great, there were no queues. He said if the stupid teachers exclude me again, we can go to LegoLand."

I'm pretty sure you can guess what he did later that morning!

The information in this book is for schools in England only, was correct at March 31st 2019 and refers to the most recent guidance which is dated September 2017.

This guidance **does not** apply to:

- Independent schools/colleges
- CTC
- City College for Technology of Arts
- 6th forms not attached to a secondary
- 16-19 Academies
- Non-maintained special schools (S41)

-but **does** apply to maintained, academies, free schools, special schools Alternative Provisions (AP) and PRUs

Acronyms and Eduspeak

Learning the lingo

Education has a language all of its own, so I've attempted to gather the most common acronyms and words/phrases (used when discussing exclusions) onto this page for reference.

Acronym/word/phrase	Meaning
PRU	Pupil Referral Unit: A centre which provides education for children who cannot go to a school
AP	Alternative Provision
LA	local authority: A government body which makes the rules in the area you live
MAT + SAT	Multi Academy Trust + Single Academy Trust
SEN (D)	Special Educational Needs (& Disabilities)
EHCA/EHCP	Education, Health and Care Assessment / Education, Health and Care Plan
SENCO	Special Educational Needs Coordinator: The person in your school who will coordinate provision for your child if they have learning difficulties to make sure they are getting the right help in school.
GB	Governing Board (or Academy Trust, or local board in Academies): A group of people in charge of setting the direction of the school. They can look at school exclusions, decisions about admissions and complaints about the school.
Headteacher (HT)	Or Principal in academies
FTE	Fixed-term exclusion
LAC	Looked-after child

Host school	The school which takes your child for a trial period or on a part-time placement.
Home school	The school which your child normally attends and is enrolled at. They maintain responsibility over your child's education.
IRP	Independent review panel
JR	Judicial Review
FTT	First Tier Tribunal
LGO	Local Government and Social Care Ombudsman - investigates complaints from the public about councils and some other bodies providing public services in England.
PSP + PBP	Pastoral Support Plan, Personal Behaviour Plan
IEP	Individual Education Plan

Context

Understanding the national picture on exclusions

If you read any of the tabloids you may be under the impression that most of England's children have received an exclusion and that there is a significant majority who are permanently excluded. Whist it is true the numbers are increasing (for a variety of reasons), it is also true that 'exclusions' are emotive, make for good reading and are reported on. It is far less likely to hit the headlines when a school has bent over backwards to accommodate children and families and avoid exclusions.

Exclusions are on the increase, but the majority of figures are lower than they were 10 years ago (2006-07). We started to get things right in 2012-13, and have gone downhill again since...

The same applies to Facebook and other support networks. If you look up exclusion, then you will find exclusion and it is easy to get a skewed view of the real situation.

As with most things in government the statistics are slow to be released. The most recent set (July 2018) covers exclusions up to the academic year 2016-17.

If you want to explore exclusions statistics in more detail, then the Department for Education (DfE) and the National Statistics Office release an updated report in the middle of July for the previous academic year. The DfE have also designed a tool for looking at local and national trends and variations which can be found at: https://department-for-education.shinyapps.io/exclusion-statistics/

Take care, this website is fascinating and several hours can disappear whilst you play with the filters available!

Here is a brief summary with some headline information:

Fixed Term Exclusions:

- Fixed Term exclusions have increased over the last academic year, from around 1786 per day to 2010.

- This is an increase from 429 in 10,000 to 476 in 10,000.

- When looking at individually named pupils this is 229 in 10,000. They receive repeated fixed-term exclusions.

- Nearly 60% of the 187,475 affected children received just one fixed-term exclusion.

- 1.5% received 10 or more separate fixed-term exclusions in the academic year.

- Since fixed term exclusions can vary in length from half a day to 45 days it is interesting to note that the average time is about 2 days (shorter than in the previous year).

- Nearly 50% of exclusions are for 1 day only and longer exclusions tend to be issued by secondary schools.

- Only 2% of fixed-term exclusions are for longer than 1 week.

- Whilst it is an increase from the previous year, compared to 2006/07 where it reached a peak, it is a decrease (5.65%).

- There are, of course variations across different types of schools, phases and within different groups (SEN, gender, ethnicity etc.)

- Over 50% of fixed-term exclusions are issued to children in Y9 or above.

Permanent Exclusions:

- Permanent exclusions have increased over the last academic year, from around 35.2 per day to 40.6.
  Bear in mind that these children do not remain 'excluded', they are readmitted to other schools, PRUs and Alternative Provisions. However, this scary number is more than 1 class a day told never to return to their school.

- When looking at individually named pupils this is an increase from 8 in 10,000 to 10 in 10,000.

- 83% of permanent exclusions come from secondary schools, where there are 20 in 10,000

- There is a difference between academies (19 in 10,000) and local authority, maintained schools (21 in 10,000). This flies in the face of reports stating that secondary academies exclude more.

- Primary school permanent exclusions have risen to 3 in 10,000

- Again, a variation exists between academies (4 in 10,000) and local authority, maintained schools (2 in 10,000)

- In special schools the trend has reversed from 8 in 10,000 to 7 in 10, 000.

- 3.5% of the pupils who receive a fixed term exclusion will go on to be permanently excluded for further offences.

- Permanent exclusions across all schools were at their lowest rates in 2012-14, with a peak in 2006/07.

- Currently, the figures remain below those of 2006/07.

Primary Schools:

- Persistent Disruptive Behaviour, Physical Assault against an Adult and Physical Assault against a Pupil are the top three reasons for fixed term exclusions in primary schools. These have slowly increased year on year and are currently at their highest levels.

- In contrast, primary school children are least likely to receive a fixed-term exclusion for theft (down to 195 children in 2016/17 from 340 in 2006/07) drugs and alcohol (45, down from 60 in 2006/07 but up from 2011/12 where only 20 offences were recorded, or sexual misconduct which remains steady at around 225 children.

- Persistent Disruptive Behaviour, Physical Assault against an Adult and Physical Assault against a Pupil are also the top three reasons for permanent exclusion in a primary school.

- The less common reasons for permanent exclusion in primary include offences classed as racism, bullying and sexual misconduct.

- Exclusions, both permanent and fixed term are on the increase for Primary schools and there is a fear that they may overtake Y9 for being the most excluded cohort.

Secondary Schools:

- Persistent Disruptive Behaviour, Other and Verbal Assault of an Adult are the top three reasons for fixed-term exclusions in a secondary school.

- Offences less commonly recorded for fixed-term exclusions are sexual misconduct, theft or damage.

- The numbers of children being excluded for theft have reduced from 8980 to 4065 and for damage 10,065 to 5290.

- Persistent Disruptive Behaviour, Other and Physical Assault on a Pupil are the most common reasons for a permanent exclusion from secondary school.

Special Schools:

- Physical Assault against an Adult, Physical Assault against a Pupil or Persistent Disruptive Behaviour result in the most fixed-term exclusions from special schools.

- Physical Assault against an Adult, Persistent Disruptive Behaviour or Other are the reasons for permanent exclusions in special schools.

- It is rare to exclude from a special school because of the nature of the students in there, however it does happen.

Pupil Characteristics:

- As usual there is the 'typical' character likely to be excluded. This child is male, has special educational needs, is eligible for and claims free school meals, is in Y9 and is likely to be of black Caribbean heritage!

- More than half of all fixed-term and permanent exclusions are issued to children in Y9 or above.

- 25% of all permanent exclusions are for pupils aged 14.

- Boys are 3 times more likely to be excluded than girls.

- Children who claim free school meals are 4 times more likely to be excluded.

- About 40% of all types of exclusions are for children who claim free school meals.

- Just under 50% of all exclusions are for children with Special Educational Needs (SEN)

- Children with SEN but no statement or EHC plan are 6 times more likely to be permanently excluded than those who are do not have SEN.

- This has increased since 2011/12 (in line with the overall increase), however the number of children with a Statement/EHCP who are permanently excluded has reduced.

- Children with an EHCP are 5 times more likely to receive a fixed-term exclusion than those who have no SEN needs, and approximately the same rate as those who have SEN without an EHC Plan.

- This has reduced since 2011/12 although the number of children who are supported without a plan have increased.

- Pupils of Gypsy Roma or Irish Traveller heritage have the highest rates of fixed term and permanent exclusions but as their population is very small the figures must be handled with caution.

Reviews:

- 560 permanent exclusions (of 7715) were reviewed in 2016/17.

- This number has increased year on year, from 320 in 2012/13.

- 525 went to independent review panels

- 350 of the decisions were upheld as correct and appropriate (67%)

- 295 requested an independent SEN witness

- 70 school governing bodies were recommended to reconsider their decision (of which 5 reinstated the pupils)

- 100 were directed to reconsider their decision of which 40 reinstated the pupils

- Therefore 45 (8%) resulted in an offer of reinstatement
- Independent review panels are not the first review that takes place, and governing bodies can make decisions to overturn the headteacher's decision.

Pupil Referral Units:

- In 2013/14 there were 349 PRUs and 12895 pupils. In 2016/17 there were 330 PRUs and 15670 pupils!
- Fixed-term exclusions account for 164.75% of the school role.
- Permanent exclusions account for 0.13%.
- There were 20 permanent exclusions from PRUs in 2016/17
- Like special schools, it is rare to permanently exclude from a PRU but not unheard of. However, those fixed term exclusion rates are scary!

Location:

- Children in the West Midlands and North West are more vulnerable to permanent exclusion (0.14%)
- The South East and Yorkshire and the Humber are least likely to permanently exclude (0.06-0.07%)
- Yorkshire and the Humber is most likely to serve a fixed-term exclusion (7.22%)
- Outer London has the lowest rate (3.49%)

On GCSE results day in 2018, a group of students 'vandalised' the Northern Line tube trains by replacing the stations map with a 'tube to prison' instead. This publicity stunt was met with two opposing opinions. The first was keen to point out the irony of their 'vandalism' which would have led to an exclusion if in school! The second were more interested in the picture presented.

(You can access the original reporting here: https://schoolsweek.co.uk/students-stage-underground-poster-campaign-against-school-exclusions/)

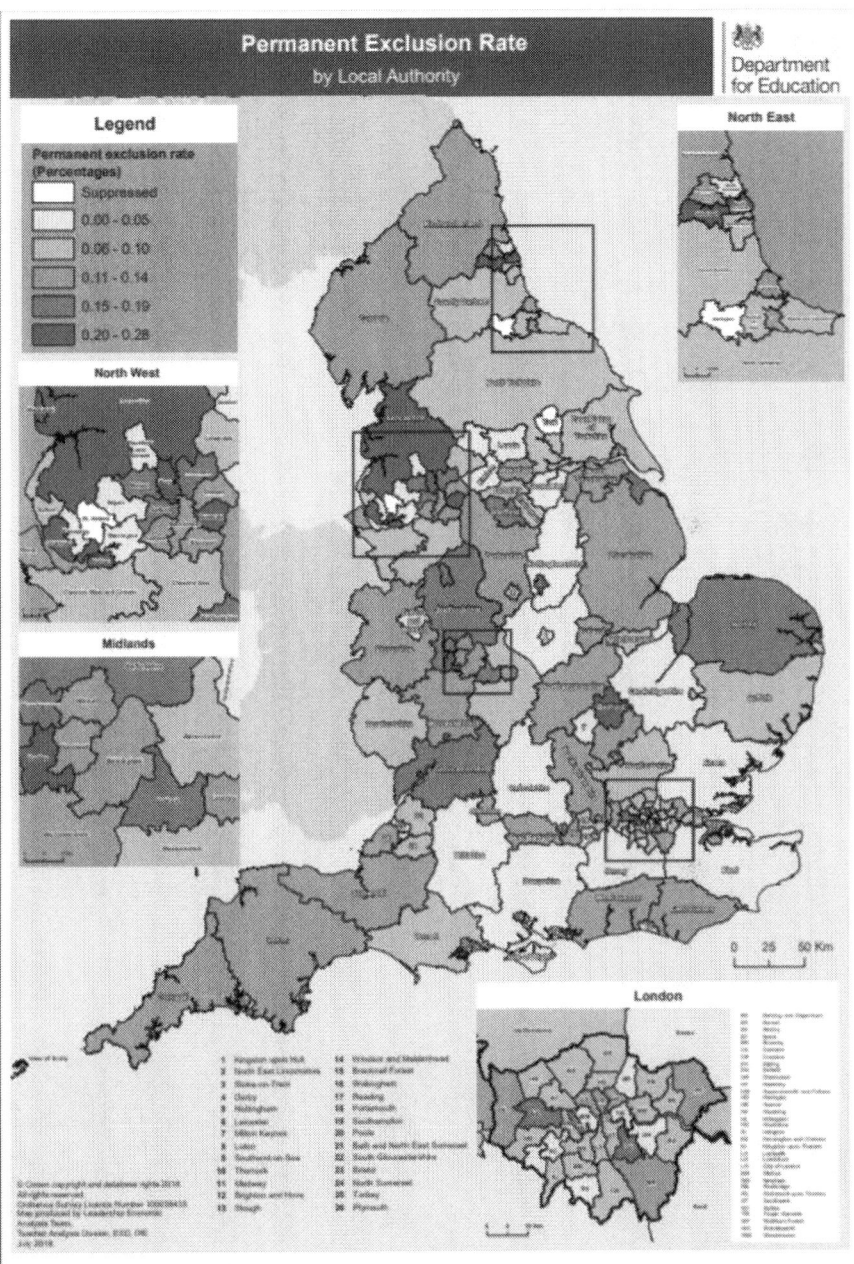

Figure 1: Permanent Exclusion by LA

Exclusions

Exclusions are underpinned by the school behaviour policy and the ethos of the school. Whereas, some operate with warm-strict philosophies (firm but fair) others use zero-tolerance and 'flattening the grass' approaches. Children who struggle to conform or push boundaries are more likely to find themselves fall foul of the latter two approaches.

When children behave badly schools have the power to 'punish them'.

Examples of punishments (sometimes called 'sanctions') include:

- a telling-off
- a letter home
- removal from a class or group (School staff can use reasonable force to control and restrain pupils. This could include leading a pupil by the arm into a classroom)
- confiscating something inappropriate for school, e.g. mobile phone or MP3 player
- detention (Schools don't have to give parents notice of after-school detentions or tell them why a detention has been given)

Eventually, some children will proceed beyond these and 'earn' an exclusion either for a single serious offence or where their behaviour has accumulated over time.

Some schools operate a system which involves issuing children with warnings for misbehaviour, which mount up and result in stricter punishments if pupils fail to improve their conduct. These penalties can culminate in a child being sent to the "consequences room", where pupils have to sit silently in booths or with a child receiving a fixed-term exclusion.

Behaviour Policies

As has already been suggested, the behaviour policy of a school is its guide indicating what students can and cannot be excluded for and the tariff of how long those exclusions are. It also sets the remit for dealing with incidents which occur outside of school.

If your child has been excluded, this should be one of the core documents you refer to. It will be on the school website or available on request. (They cannot refuse to give you a copy.)

As with pretty much everything in education, schools are given guidance on what they should include in their behaviour policies. The document for this is on the DfE Website with the exciting title, "Behaviour and Discipline in Schools – January 2016". It is a deceptively thin guide considering everything it underpins; however, it makes good use of signposting the reader to further guidance in other publications.

A brief summary of the guidance is included here as it drives the exclusions process and ethos of the school.

1. Behaviour policies seek to promote good behaviour, self-discipline and respect. They have a role in preventing bullying and ensuring that students complete work. They are used to regulate conduct.

2. A behaviour policy may include reference to the school's screening and searching policies, reasonable force, restraint and physical contact, powers beyond the school gate and pastoral care systems.

3. They should identify the school rules and disciplinary penalty for breaking those rules.

4. The guidance refers to teacher's powers to discipline, impose sanctions and confiscate pupil items.

5. The guidance suggests different sanctions that can be imposed including detention and the use of isolation rooms as a punishment.

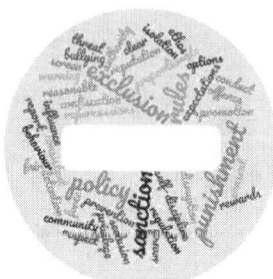

In essence, if it is in the school policy then the school is able to issue penalties for non-compliance. Whilst we would expect those penalties to be less punitive than an exclusion, repeated offences may lead to an exclusion over what is suggested in the policy.

We would expect to see:

- A verbal warning
- Extra work assigned or repetition until it is of acceptable standard
- Setting of written tasks as punishment
- Loss of privileges
- Missing break time (although time has to be given for a toilet break and to eat)
- Detention, including lunch, after-school or weekends
- School based community service
- Time in a sanction room/isolation
- Being 'on report'
- As a final resort, or accumulating in exclusion

I write this in the month where Twitter has been going crazy over 'Ban the Booths'. A reference to sanction rooms where children are sent, in some cases for many days at a time. As you'll discover, I often sit on the fence with these discussions. The alternative is exclusion. Many of the students I have worked with actually 'enjoy' their time in the sanction rooms, feeling that the atmosphere is more laid back, they get more work done, it is quieter (especially environmentally as they tend not to have over busy classroom displays) and there is a member of staff to a relatively low number of pupils. I'd even dare to say it's a little like the parent who treats their child when excluded…some students will misbehave in lesson in order to get sent back to the room as they 'prefer' it!

Who can exclude a child from school?

s52 (1) Education Act 2002 – a headteacher of a LA maintained school may exclude a pupil from the school for a fixed period or permanently

The only person with the authority to exclude a child from school is the headteacher. In their absence the nominated Deputy Head can take that decision.

Who is chosen to convey the message to you that your child is excluded, is for the school to decide. In my experience, it is usually someone the family has a good relationship with or someone you have met before. Therefore, it is not uncommon for you to receive the message, "I am excluding X for 3 days," from their Head of Year/House, tutor, class teacher or SENCO. However, they will not have made the actual decision and will be acting on the instruction of the headteacher.

It isn't the easiest thing to do – sit in a room with a family whom you have built up a trusting relationship and have to inform them that their child has breached the school policies and are now facing an exclusion. Especially as we may often have been the advocate for the child in a meeting prior to the parents arriving where we were fighting for them not to be excluded. However, in the parent meeting we have to show we tow the company line and not display that we may disagree with the decision that has been made! As a parent, we know you are upset but please:

Don't shoot the messenger!

What can a child be excluded for?

Removal from school by exclusion should be to:
* Protect the health and safety of the individual
* Protect the health and safety of others
or
* Prevent the disruption to learning
They Never Give Up On You (Children's Commissioner) p21

Nell repeatedly refuses to follow staff instructions and requests. She disrupts the learning of her class by making the teacher (and class) wait for her. Nell can legally be excluded for persistent disruption to learning.

A child can be excluded for <u>anything</u> that is considered disciplinary grounds.

The school **MUST** have a behaviour policy and that will include the school's rules and disciplinary penalties for breaking the rules. This will be available on the school website, or, where it is an academy, on the school or trust website or available on request.

A behaviour policy will usually include sections on screening and searching pupils, the power to use reasonable force, the power to discipline beyond the school gate and the sanctions applied to various misdemeanours.

Sanctions are the 'punishments' given by schools when rules are broken. They can (legally) include (as listed on page 22)

- A verbal reprimand
- Extra work or repetition until it is of acceptable standard

- Setting of written tasks as punishment (unbelievably this includes lines)
- Loss of privileges (such as being a prefect, or involvement in a non-uniform day)
- Missing break time
- Detention, including lunch, after-school or weekends
- School based community service (e.g. litter picking)
- Time in a sanction room
- Being 'on report'
- Or, exclusion.

---

3 BEHAVIOUR THAT MAY RESULT IN EXCLUSION

3.1 Exclusion may be considered appropriate for incidents that occur:

- On school premises
- While travelling to and from school
- On supervised visits from school
- At any other such time, where the incident is clearly linked to the school

3.2 The list below sets out a range of incidents for which exclusion may be considered appropriate:

- Verbal abuse towards a member of staff
- Physical aggression towards a member of staff or another pupil
- Threatening or bullying behaviour
- Refusal to accept school rules
- Refusal to follow instructions
- Possession of dangerous weapons.
- Theft
- Damage to property
- Sexually related incidents
- Action that brings the school into disrepute
- Racial incidents
- Smoking during school hours, including travelling to and from school
- Any other incident deemed serious by the headteacher
- Possession of illegal substances (see 3.3)

3.3 The Governing Body has agreed that there should be 'zero tolerance' with regard to illegal substances. Any pupil found to be possessing, receiving, taking or supplying illegal substances during school hours, including while travelling to and from school will result in permanent exclusion.

3.4 The Headteacher may also notify the police of incidents that involve a breach of current legislation.

Figure 2: Extract from a Secondary school policy

Whatever the sanction delivered it has to be a **proportionate** and **fair response** which can vary according to the age of the child and any other special circumstances that affect the child (e.g. SEN, bereavement, caring responsibilities.)

A punishment must be proportionate. In determining whether a punishment is reasonable, section 91 of the Education and Inspections Act 2006 says the penalty must be reasonable in all the circumstances and that account must be taken of the child's age, any special educational needs or disability they may have, and any religious requirements affecting them.

Sanctions cannot breach any other legislation, such as special educational needs, race and other equalities and human rights.

Some schools will use a tariff system, whereby lesser offences (sometimes called C1) involve verbal warnings and more serious offences (e.g. C5) result in exclusions or removal to a sanction room. They may serve similar tariffs for the types of exclusions too. Where verbal abuse of a member of staff might be a 1-day exclusion, physical assault could be 3 days. These are entirely for the school to decide upon.

As the SENCO in my school. I was often asked to discuss exclusions with parents. Before the meeting, I would be advocating for the child in a conversation with the headteacher and other staff involved. Where our tariff might have stated a 3-day exclusion, I was often able to argue that whilst a sanction was necessary, a shorter exclusion would be more appropriate and accommodate the child's understanding and needs.

It would be lawful for a school to exclude for:

- Repeated failure to follow academic instructions
- Failure to complete behaviour sanctions (e.g. detentions)
- Repeated and persistent breach of the school behaviour policy – even where the individual offence would not have been sufficient to warrant an exclusion.
- A persistent breach of policy where other strategies have been exhausted or are inappropriate
- A serious one-off offence

There are 12 categories of exclusion

Physical Assault against a Pupil
- fighting
- violent behaviour
- wounding
- obstruction and jostling

Physical Assault against an Adult
- violent behaviour
- wounding
- obstruction and jostling

Bullying
- verbal
- physical
- homophobic bullying
- racist bullying

Verbal Abuse/Threatening behaviour against a Pupil
- threatened violence
- aggressive behaviour
- swearing
- homophobic abuse and harassment
- verbal intimidation
- carrying an offensive weapon

Verbal Abuse/Threatening behaviour against an Adult
- threatened violence
- aggressive behaviour
- swearing
- homophobic abuse and harassment
- verbal intimidation
- carrying an offensive weapon

Racist Abuse
- racist taunting and harassment
- derogatory racist statements
- swearing that can be attributed to racist characteristics
- racist bullying
- racist graffiti

Sexual Misconduct
- sexual abuse
- sexual assault
- sexual harassment
- lewd behaviour
- sexual bullying
- sexual graffiti

Drug & Alcohol related
- possession of illegal drugs
- inappropriate use of prescribed drugs
- drug dealing
- smoking
- alcohol abuse
- substance abuse

Damage:
Includes damage to school or personal property belonging to any member of the school community
- vandalism
- arson
- graffiti

Theft
- stealing school property
- stealing personal property (pupil or adult)
- stealing from local shops on a school outing
- selling and dealing in stolen property

Persistent Disruptive behaviour
- challenging behaviour
- disobedience
- persistent violation of school rules

Other
Includes incidents which are not covered by the categories above, but this category should be used sparingly.

Persistent Disruption

My eldest son doesn't attend the best of schools! I recently asked him how much of each lesson is disrupted by other students and he estimated 20 minutes of every lesson, every day was lost to dealing with regular offenders. This means that 1/3 of every year is lost. Or, as he is in Year 11, he has been held back to the same amount of teaching that a Year 9 would have received without interruption. With this in mind, it is not surprising that when children persistently misbehave school's take action.

So, what is persistent disruption? It could be shouting out, talking over the teacher, not being prepared for the lesson (no pen or book), refusing to sit where asked or arriving late (without a justifiable reason). Whilst it is of no doubt that the teacher can control much of this with engaging lessons, clear expectations and early intervention, where these are unsuccessful then there is likely to be an underlying cause.

Oddly enough my 'worst' lessons were not Friday afternoons following a wet lunch, but the lesson between morning break and lunchtime each day. Why? Many of my students didn't bring a morning snack and by this time they were hungry or to coin a modern phrase "hangry". No matter how engaging the lesson they struggled to concentrate, fell easily off task and generally 'disrupted learning'. As someone who likes their food, I completely understand how they felt! Toast, biscuits, cereal bars and hot chocolate have played a large part in addressing my classroom behaviour management across all ages.

There will, however, be some students where their needs are met, but they just don't want to play by the rules (perhaps they just hate the subject). These students may hit the school threshold for persistent disruption and find themselves on the receiving end of an exclusion. Schools are left with few options when the subject is compulsory, although in secondary allowing the student to drop something non-statutory for a more favourable option may help to eliminate the difficulties. I say this hesitatingly, since our young man who was promised the Alton Towers trip by Dad was allowed to drop one of his options, replacing it with supported study time…he then began disrupting in another subject using the theory he could get out of this too!

They cannot be excluded for...

So, the school can exclude for anything they consider to be a disciplinary offence...but what can they NOT use as a reason for exclusion?

1. The behaviour of the parents. They can refuse to have you on the school site, but they cannot refuse to educate your child.

Nell's mum threatened the headteacher last week. She was under the influence of alcohol and screamed abuse at the head across the playground before marching up to her, poking her in the chest and spitting in her face. Nell cannot be excluded for her mother's behaviour. The school can, however, ban the Nell's mother from the premises.

Nell's mother also has a younger child in the nursery. The school might opt to be helpful and collect/deliver the child to and from the school gate, but they are not obliged to do so. Nell's mother will need to make separate arrangements.

2. An academic reason. Your child may not be academically achieving as well as they want. They are not allowed to exclude for this reason.

Nell is failing in her subjects. She is not making the progress expected. She cannot be excluded for this reason.

3. They cannot meet your child's needs. This would be discrimination and it is discussed in detail later.

53% of surveyed parents said their child had been excluded because the school acknowledged there was a lack of staff that day to look after them. These were planned exclusions, for example where their TA was attending a course. 49% of those stated it happened on a regular basis, even weekly. These are unlawful exclusions and are discriminating against the child for their medical or disability related needs.

4. A behaviour related to their special educational need.

Tom has learning difficulties and also has motor and vocal tics. He is on the school SEN register as having Tourette's. His medical reports clearly state that he uses obscene language and gestures. Tom cannot be excluded for swearing during a tic attack.

5. You or your child does not meet specific conditions before being reinstated. (See the examples in the box below.)

Tom's father works long 12-hour shifts from 7am to 7pm. Tom has just completed a 3-day exclusion. The school is unable to arrange a reintegration meeting with his father in attendance. They must not extend his exclusion.

6. Your child's friends or classmates did something, but your child was not involved. Your child cannot be excluded for association (although if they didn't make a reasonable attempt to stop it or report it, then the school may choose to punish them another way.)

7. Turning up in the wrong uniform (as a one-off.) A school can exclude for persistent/repeated offences with the school uniform, and they can send a child home to "change". Where extreme breaches exist (e.g. haircuts in direct opposition to the school's stated policy) then an exclusion might be issued.

Tom turns up to school with tramlines cut into his hair. This is in breach of the school's behaviour policy. He is given a 3-day fixed-term exclusion. On his return the tramlines are still visible (he has slow-growing hair!) The school cannot exclude him for a further period.

8. Coming to school late (as a one-off). Where a child is persistently late to school, they may accrue an exclusion, but it is more commonly dealt with using detentions to make up the missed time. Exclusion defeats the object!

9. Their safety. A school cannot exclude a child for their own safety, for example where they are being bullied and it is suggested they 'stay at home'. However, where a child is self-harming or putting other children/staff in an unsafe situation then an exclusion might be appropriate.

It is never appropriate to exclude for minor infringements of school rules, such as a breach of uniform or wearing jewellery, especially where such rules may disadvantage one gender or certain ethnic groups, faiths or cultures.
They Never Give Up On You (Children's Commissioner) p21

What a school cannot say (and I've heard all of them at some point!)

- Your child does not fit very well at our school, perhaps you'd like to move them.

- We cannot meet the level of needs your child exhibits.

- Did you know the school around the corner has lots of children like Nell?

- You might like to look at other schools to avoid an exclusion.

- We don't make adjustments to our behaviour policy, everyone follows the same rules

- We excluded your older child; it probably isn't a good idea for the younger one to come here

- Oh, yes, we've heard about this one's reputation. This probably isn't the best school.

- Have you been to look at school X? They're really good with children like…

- You can't use SEN as an excuse.

- We'll just send Tom home early to cool off, don't worry, we won't record it as an exclusion.

- We're sorry Nell is being bullied. It might be a good idea to keep her at home so you can make sure she's safe.

- We are issuing a part-time timetable for Tom.

- Nell is not making sufficient academic progress if she doesn't improve, we will exclude her.

- You haven't attended a reintegration meeting so Tom cannot come back to school.

- As a parent we have banned you from the school site, so it would be better if you took your child elsewhere.

- Relationships have broken down, maybe you'd like to move elsewhere or keep Nell off school.

- We don't have any staff to support Tom on Friday, so can you keep him at home?

- We know that Nell doesn't like change. Her teacher is off tomorrow. Maybe you want to keep her off too?
- We have some special visitors in school, if they see how badly Tom behaves there could be a lot of trouble and we will have to exclude him. It might be a good idea if he has tummy ache tomorrow.

It didn't happen in school...

The headteacher has the ability to exclude a child for behaviour that did not take place on the school grounds or during school hours. Generally, it is used for incidents that bring the school into disrepute and the most common examples pertain to when a child is travelling to or from school in uniform and does something 'wrong'. For example: shoplifting or being abusive to other bus passengers.

The types of incidents which may be considered should be clearly indicated in the school behaviour policy. Usually it will include reference to being in school uniform, travelling to and from school, obviously identifiable as a student from the school (e.g. on a school visit/work experience) or involved in a school activity off site. It will clearly indicate that the behaviour may bring the school's name into disrepute (and adverse reputation), poses a threat to the school or may have continuing repercussions.

I once had a student involved in dealing drugs outside of school. He was arrested, charged and released. The school felt it was unable to ensure that he wasn't dealing on the school site (despite regular searches) and took the decision to exclude him (remaining in school would seriously harm the welfare of other pupils). As he was Y11, we used a fixed-term exclusion and allowed him back on site into a separate location to undertake his examinations.

Examples:

Poor behaviour on a school visit	Bullying via social media at the weekend
Damage to neighbouring properties on the way home from school	Damage to a staff member's front garden following a phone call home for poor behaviour in class!

Tom went on the school trip to the farm. He was asked repeatedly not to touch the animals in the lambing area. He ignored his teacher's instructions. When one of the farm workers asked him to move away from the fence, he swore at him and threw a bucket hitting one of the lambs.

Nell also went on a school trip to the farm. She didn't like the sandwiches her Mum had packed for her and was in a 'bad mood'. The children were offered the chance to hold baby chickens. Nell seemed to be calm. The teacher told the group that they would need to put the chicks back in the hay and wash their hands for lunch. Nell was not happy. She threw the baby chick and in the process of storming out of the barn she knocked over one of her classmates who dropped their chick and Nell stomped on it! Once, we may have called an accident...jumping up and down on it several times was probably not.

Tom used the filters on Instagram to make Nell look like a pig over the weekend. He then posted this on his Facebook page saying that this was a more lifelike representation, oink oink. When Nell returned to school all her peers were making 'oink' sounds instead of talking to her.

Tom sent a 'dick pic' to Nell and asked her to be his girlfriend. She told her parents who reported it to the school. The school informed the police (sorry, it's distribution of child pornography...against the law) and they decided no further action was necessary after explaining things to Tom. His parents confiscated his phone and put child safety measures on other forms of electronic communication along with grounding him! Nell didn't let things drop and started to post nasty comments on social media referring to sizes and shapes. Although she didn't post the picture (she too would be guilty of distribution of child pornography if she had) there was no doubt as to what she was alluding to. As a result, Tom's friends began to tease him. Nell was given an exclusion from school for inciting bullying.

Nell decided it would be a good idea to kick down all the picket fences in the street next to the school on her way home last night. No reason, she just felt like it.

Tom truanted from school by crawling under the fence at the back of the field. The field backed on to a series of houses. Tom was spotted by the owner of the house who reported it to the school. By the time Tom got home, the school were waiting to take him back. On the way home that night, Tom acquired a can of paint from the gentleman's garden shed and poured it all over his garden furniture. (Caught by a mobile phone video taken by his friend and posted on YouTube!)

Nell was disruptive in lesson, throwing pencils and shouting out. Her teacher made a phone call home to her family and asked if there was any particular issues she needed to be aware of. The family said there was nothing different. The teacher decided not to sanction Nell but to see if she behaved differently the following lesson. That night, the teacher, who lived local to the school, heard a disturbance outside her house and saw Nell smashing her plant pots and garden ornaments (including gnomes) and stamping on her flowers.

Nell was not the most productive in my science lessons. She would do anything to get out of working. I informed her father of this at parents' evening and he was not impressed (similar reports from other teachers). When I left school that night my car window was smashed. CCTV footage showed Nell come back to the school and throw one of the decorative rocks through my window. Mine was the only car parked at the front of the school.

All real examples and I have never taken children to a farm or zoo since the chicken incident.

What are the different types of exclusion?

Officially there are two types of exclusion. Permanent and Fixed-term.

I'm old-school, born in the 70s and educated through to the early 90s.

Permanent exclusion was called being 'expelled' or expulsion. In very simple terms, it's the same as being fired from your job. You leave the premises and are not permitted to return again.

Fixed-term exclusions were called 'suspensions'. You were sent home and your educational opportunities suspended or put on hold for a period of time.

We also had, back in the day, some rather dodgy practice around 'cooling off'. Being sent home to calm down and returning the following day for a fresh start. This type of exclusion is now unlawful. If a school sends a child home early it cannot be for a cooling off period and must be recorded as an exclusion (or medical, ill etc.).

As a parent and a SENCO, I'm controversially on the fence here.

I believe, that some children can get themselves into such a state of adrenalin fuelled anxiety that keeping them in school is asking for trouble. But they don't warrant an exclusion we simply want to avoid that from being the case. I've known students coming down from the adrenaline burst that follows a major incident, vomit everywhere!

I would argue for allowing those students home on 'medical' (ill) grounds with the agreement of the parents and the child involved.

I would, unfortunately, be giving the child an unlawful exclusion if I suggested this.

Permanent exclusions can be issued for single serious offences, however, there have generally been some smaller incidents in the lead up to a permanent exclusion for the vast majority of children.

Fixed-term exclusions can be given for anything from half a day to 45 days. They are accumulated over the course of a year and tipping over the 45-day mark (or 15 days in a term) could lead to consideration of 'persistency' and the issuing of a permanent exclusion.

Lunch time exclusions are still exclusions and have to be recorded as such. In fact, a lunch time exclusion means the child accumulates a half day exclusion each time (5 days over two weeks).

Part-time timetables are frowned upon as every child is entitled to a full-time education. For some children, for example those with a health difficulty which prevents them accessing education all day without becoming tired, they can be appropriate. For other children who show high levels of anxiety (which may manifest as behaviour that challenges) they can also be used. However, they should never be viewed as a long-term solution and should be reviewed regularly with a view to increasing the hours up to full-time as soon as possible. Parents do not have to agree to part-time timetables.

Need to check what your child's exclusion record looks like?

Ask for a print of their attendance. The vast majority of systems use / and \ to mark morning and afternoon presence. You are looking for '**E**' for exclusions. Any other code should be explained but must not be used if your child is being excluded.

An **E** is an authorised absence. Regardless of the fact the school has told the child not to attend it is still an absence and it will count against attendance percentages. However, it is an authorised absence, so the school cannot threaten you with attendance fines where the exclusions are what cause the reduced figure. (Just be careful of other absences from school as these are not 'protected' in the same way.)

Where your child has a part-time timetable, the code for the sessions where they are not in school is **C**, authorised circumstance. The other codes commonly seen are **D** where a child has dual registration at two establishments and the **D** denotes they are expected to be marked /\ at the other site. Or **B** which is used for 'educated off-site'. This is not being given work to complete at home, but more, for example a tutor is sent to work with them or they are enrolled in an online course where their presence and participation is monitored. In other words, they are not just accessing Show My Homework, My Maths or similar but are sat in 'virtual classrooms' such as EdLounge or Nisai.

Covert exclusions

Covert exclusions are unlawful. They exist where a school colludes to record an absence with a different code and include informal, cooling off periods or persuading the family that the child would be better off opting to come home for lunches.

Sometimes families feel that the school is doing them a favour in not 'excluding' their child but in essence it just delays your entitlement to legal processes. You can't complain about your child being sent home (excluded) if they haven't been recorded as an exclusion. The formal exclusions process, meetings and complaints system do not fall into place until real exclusions are recorded.

Examples of covert exclusions:

- Cooling off – 'take him home and let him calm down, don't worry we won't mark it as an absence'. 62% of surveyed parents said that they had been told this.

- Going home early – 'if you collect him at 2:30 then he won't get into trouble'. 70% of surveyed parents explained that they had been told their child was having a 'bad day'

- Lunch times – 'it would be a much better idea if he went home for lunch, don't you think?' 86.4% of parents explained that they had been asked to do this and it was not recorded as an exclusion.

- "I think Tom would be better at another school and perhaps it is in his best interests not to come back here whilst you are sorting that out. We'll give you some work to do with him at home and we won't mark it as an exclusion, then the other school doesn't need to know about it."

If your child is being excluded,
make sure that the school is marking it as an exclusion.

How long can an exclusion be for?

A permanent exclusion is just that, permanent (except where a reinstatement is proposed following appeal.)

A single fixed-term exclusion can be half a day (minimum) to 45 days (maximum). Shorter periods of 'exclusion', for example an hour or a lunch break, are each recorded as half a day.

Exclusions are usually issued in blocks of time; however, they can be non-continuous. For example, lunchtime exclusions only prevent the child being in school over lunch...they attend either side of this.

Students can be excluded multiple times in an academic year up to a total of 45 days. Where pupils move school part-way through an academic year, their previous tally of exclusions will follow them.

Once you have been told how long an exclusion is for, it **cannot** be **extended** or **converted** except in **exceptional circumstances**.

CIRCUMSTANCES TO EXTEND/CONVERT

Fixed term – extension	*New or additional evidence comes to light.*
	A second exclusion can be issued to run straight after the first.
Permanent – conversion	*New or additional evidence comes to light.*
	Often where this is likely to happen, the school will have issued a 5-day pending permanent exclusion notice to the family.
	A permanent exclusion can be issued to start immediately after the end of the fixed-term.

Tom was excluded for a fight at lunchtime. He was given a 1-day exclusion for the following day. That evening, the cleaners discovered that one of the toilets had been destroyed. On examining the CCTV footage and investigating further, it turns out Tom was guilty. His family are contacted, and a second exclusion of 1-day is served to be completed immediately after the first.

Before making the decision to exclude a child it should have been investigated thoroughly so the grounds of 'new or additional evidence' being presented should be rare.

Exclusion for an INDEFINITE period is unlawful.

Fixed Term Exclusions

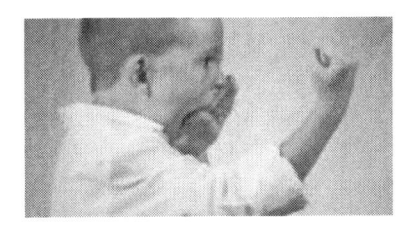

A fixed term exclusion can be set for half a day up to 45 days. Anything shorter than half a day must be recorded as a half day.

If illegal 'cooling off' exclusions were correctly recorded as fixed-term exclusions, then the fixed-term exclusion figures would make for even more bleak reading.

The most common fixed-term exclusions issued are for just 1 or 2 days in both primary and secondary schools. For greater offences a 5-day exclusion is given. It is uncommon to see single exclusions of greater than 5 days and where they do exist, they tend to be issued by secondary schools just prior to term breaks/holidays.

Fixed-term exclusions indicate the behaviour or the accumulation of behaviours has gone beyond what the school believes can be dealt with using other sanctions.

With a fixed-term exclusion the child returns to their own school at the end of the period to carry on with their education.

Regardless of the length of this exclusion the school should provide work. If it is 5 days or less then they provide it directly it is 6 days or more in one block then the school has to provide an alternative (full-time) education from day 6 onwards. This may be a placement in a PRU or Alternative Provision, or it could take the form of virtual education and tutors.

Fixed-Term pending Permanent Exclusions

Very rarely a school may want to permanently exclude a student but the investigation into circumstances surrounding the incident is taking longer than they feasibly have and they don't want the student on the site whilst the investigation is concluded. A little like being suspended from work pending an investigation into gross misconduct which then results in you being fired from your job, a school may decide to issue a 5-day-pending-permanent exclusion. This exclusion is not mentioned in any of the guidance and yet nearly every school spoken to will confirm that this is something they would do if they needed to check their facts, take legal advice or consider additional information.

Nell attacked Tom in the corridor before school. Tom has an autistic spectrum condition and Nell had suffered a serious brain trauma 18 months earlier. The attack was unprecedented. Nell had not displayed this kind of behaviour before, although she had been rather more stroppy and sulky over the last few months. Tom and Nell had been in the same classes for 4 years and although not friends they were not enemies either. The attack on Tom was sustained and even when he was curled up in a foetal ball crying for help and asking her to stop, she continued stamping on his head and kicking him. As the bell went for lessons, she picked up her bag and calmly walked away.

The school was left with a dilemma. Tom was admitted to hospital, although there was no lasting physical damage other than bruising. Nell showed no remorse. When shown the CCTV footage, she laughed when Tom started crying.

To complicate matters for the school, Nell is a looked-after child. Wherever possible they need to avoid a permanent exclusion. However, the attack had frightened the other children in the school and there was no way to separate Tom and Nell in classes. The school issued a 5-day pending permanent exclusion, whilst they took advice from the virtual head (the person who looks after looked-after children), social care, and the brain-injury team at the hospital amongst others.

In this case, Nell was admitted to another school on a managed move. She was successful and transferred to their school role after the 6-week trial period. A permanent exclusion was not issued.

I know of one school who were really struggling with the behaviour of one student. They had exhausted all available resources in supporting him and the final straw was him running up to an elderly visitor in the school and stealing her crutches (she fell) before proceeding to run up and down the corridor shouting, "I'm cured!" The school was understandably embarrassed and felt that given all the support he received this was the end. They placed him on a 5-day-pending-permanent exclusion. Whilst they were considering their final decision, he wrote a letter of apology to the elderly lady, who was very touched by his honesty. As the letter hadn't been prompted by the school, they decided to give him one final chance. (He didn't quite manage a 'pure' record after the event, but it seemed to have been the wake-up call he needed...he now works in a care home for the elderly and loves 'entertaining' the individuals.)

Permanent Exclusions

In response to a serious breach or persistent breaches of schools behaviour policy
AND
where allowing the pupil to remain in school would seriously harm the education OR welfare of the pupil or others in the school

Where a school issues a permanent exclusion, it is because they believe there are no other options.

I will admit to having worked in a school where we desperately needed a special school place for a particular student (with a statement, the old equivalent of an EHC Plan). He really wasn't coping, and no services were listening to us, the family or the child. In the end, after his third day of running riot around the school and leaping from one building roof to another in his attempt at parkour or sitting on the roof smoking and setting fire to the random debris blown up there, we felt we could not keep him safe. Fixed-term exclusions had no effect other than to cause further stress to his mother and transfer the problem from school to the community. We took the decision that a permanent exclusion was our only option for his (and our safety). Amazingly, the local authority found a place in a special school for him that afternoon. (With the right support he managed to modify his behaviour and joined the army at age 18, he's now 26 and enjoying his tours of the world. He admits he's still a little reckless at times, but the structure of the armed forces allows him to expend his energy whilst being under strict control!)

This is not an ideal situation for any party to be in and certainly not a justifiable use of permanent exclusions, however it goes to illustrate that as a school we had tried everything in our power to support the young man and were left with no further options.

Whilst the fixed-term exclusions have a strict set of processes that should be followed a permanent exclusion has additional elements.

1. The headteacher sends a letter without delay to parents. This could be given at the time of the exclusion by hand although it is more likely to follow in the post the following day. If a parent has signed up to receive communications by email then the notification can be issued electronically, although it is standard procedure to follow this up with a traditional letter.

2. The headteacher informs governors of the school and the home local authority of the child. The home local authority is the one in which the child lives. This is important where schools take children from several local authorities or where the child is looked-after.

3. The home local authority is responsible for organising alternative provision from day 6. This might be placement in a PRU (pupil referral unit), a home tutor or online education package or placement in an alternative provision that is not a school. The choice of what is provided belongs with the local authority.

4. The governing body must convene a meeting within 15 days to discuss the exclusions. The parents are invited attend along with their child if they wish. The meeting is convened to the availability of the governors and not to the convenience of the parents. If you are unable to attend, then any parental written representations you choose to make must be read at the meeting.

5. At the governing body meeting, they will decide if the school has followed its own procedures and behaviour policy correctly. The governing body can overturn the headteachers' decision. If they uphold the decisions, then the parents can take the exclusion to an IRP (independent review panel)

6. Where the child's behaviour is a result of parenting, or lack of, then the school or local authority could ask for a parenting contract or ask the magistrates court to make a parenting order. I have to admit I've never seen this happen in any of my schools – who am I to judge someone else's parenting?

Alternatives

A school behaviour policy makes it clear what sanctions they will use. Exclusion really is the last resort for the vast majority of establishments.

LEVEL OF SANCTION

One off, minor incidents of disruption in lessons or inappropriate behaviour will normally attract sanctions such as a verbal rebuke, isolation for a short period or detention. More serious incidents of disruption or misbehaviour may well result in isolation or exclusion. Unless there are very exceptional circumstances, any student verbally abusing, intimidating or assaulting a member of staff will be excluded. If a student repeats inappropriate behaviour or persistently disrupts the learning of others, the seriousness of the sanction will, under normal circumstances, increase. The Academy will make reasonable adjustments under the Equality Act 2010, in respect of safeguarding and students with special educational needs (SEN).

Policy from a school referencing reasonable adjustments and the Equality Act.

A school has a selection of options when it comes to alternatives to exclusion, although not all are appropriate to each individual and not all are available to every school.

Some of the options are outlined on the following pages, but, with the exception of Early intervention, it does not mean that your school will (or has to) offer them.

Early Intervention

Early intervention should pick up on issues before there is ever a need to exclude a child. We know there will always be serious one-off incidents which need an exclusion, but the vast majority have a build-up.

My personal opinion is that no child should ever have to be excluded for persistent disruption…it is a clear indication that their needs are not being met or addressed. I'm also of the feeling that any child who receives an exclusion for any reason should be flagged to the SENCO even where no SEN issues are known to exist. A good SENCO will be able to spot the triggers or antecedents and help put in place a plan to try and ensure it doesn't happen again.

Following an exclusion, the reintegration meeting is essential in looking at what happened, why, and ensuring it doesn't reoccur. Sadly, reintegration meetings are not compulsory and often poorly conducted with schools simply laying down the policy with a 'telling off' and 'this cannot happen again' without actually addressing any underlying issues.

Where a school has a concern about a child and believes they are on the road to exclusion they should be pooling all their available resources in order to make sure the route is diverted. I've worked in many schools where resources are scarce and although in the ideal world we'd be pulling in an assessment by an educational psychologist and support from the local authority behaviour specialists, this isn't always possible. I throw this back to the SENCO who should have a basic toolkit and knowledge to be able to advise.

The Common Assessment Framework (CAF) was an excellent document for gathering all information in one place and the subsequent Team Around the Child (TAC) meeting put all professionals in one room to offer support and ideas. Whilst not as commonly used, the principles remain. A CAF will look at wider family issues that can impact on behaviour in school. Families can find it difficult to share these but as they are having an impact on the child and their behaviour it is important to be as open as possible.

Things going on at home might include:

- Homelessness or risk of losing the home/moving house
- Bereavement or serious illness of close relatives or family friends
- Family disputes (including divorce, domestic abuse, arguments, siblings in trouble)
- Financial worries
- Exposure to undesirable influences: drugs, alcohol, abuse

As a result of the assessment the team should be able to make reasonable adjustments in school to policies or procedures or to recommend additional or different support in order to meet needs. This whole process is sometimes referred to as a multi-agency assessment.

Where a child has recognised special educational needs, these should be reviewed and in the case of a child with an Education, Health and Care Plan an early or interim/emergency review may need to be held to address concerns.

Part-time Timetables

Children are entitled to a full-time education.

Legally, full-time education is only defined for child maintenance payments and claiming child benefits and is more than 12 hours a week in supervised study, this allows for study at college or university where the remaining time is considered to be self-study.

It is generally taken that children spend about 5 hours a day in school lesson (i.e. not in collective worship, assemblies, registration, and any breaks or time between lessons which are not included) and therefore full-time education is usually considered to be 25 hours. Taking the DFES (defunct since 2007) guidance for Key Stage 1 being 21 hours, and Key Stage 2 being 23.5 hours, we can conclude that a full-time education is between 21 and 25 hours. Early years are not included since they are not of compulsory school age.

Sometimes, a school may suggest a child attends school part-time. This could be to allow the child to recover from being unwell, be a short-term solution until more suitable support can be arranged or be part of a planned phased return to school after a child has been off school.

If your child is struggling to attend school you can talk to the school about them attending only some lessons, and then discuss how they could be supported to gradually increase their time in school.

Part-time education should only be a short-term solution as a way of improving things for a child. Schools should not provide a part-time timetable as a way of managing a pupil's additional support needs. Long-term part-time attendance might be a sign that the right support is not in place for a child or they are not attending the right school.

The law says that "pupils are to be educated as far as is reasonable in accordance with wishes of their parents." This means that if you do not want to agree to a part-time timetable then you do not have to. If the school is suggesting your child attends part-time, they should ask you if are happy with this arrangement and involve you in planning. If the school is saying they are unable to have your child full-time and you do not agree with the idea of part-time attendance, the school must follow formal exclusion procedures in order for your child to be out of school. If your child is in secondary school, it is worth discussing how a part-time timetable will affect their subject choices and exams.

One key thing to consider is your child's access to wider activities in school when they are not full-time. So, for example, if the class is taking a trip to a museum, will your child also be attending on an extended day. If the answer is yes, then why can they not attend full-time on a more regular basis. If the answer is no, then how will the school ensure that they do not miss out on every trip/event.

Organising a part-time timetable is much easier in a primary school where the student will attend for just part of the day (usually the morning) and access their core subjects (English and Maths). As primary schools usually have only one teacher per class it is easier to ensure continuity of subjects. Many primary pupils faced with this will miss out of the less academic 'fun' subjects generally delivered in the afternoon – for example, art, PE and science.

In secondary schools, a part-time timetable might involve being in school full-time but only attending some subjects. Make sure there is a clear plan for what will be done in this 'spare time' and what any long-term impact will be. Often called 'dropping a subject' it is used to support academic progress as much as prevent exclusions and is more common in Key Stage 4 (Years 10 and 11).

In secondary schools where the school is proposing (for example) mornings only, how will your child keep up with the work missed in the afternoons? It is common with this scenario for students to miss 1 or 2 or their English/Maths lessons a week and have sporadic attendance in those subjects making it difficult to stay on track and inevitably ends up with behavioural incidents becoming more likely.

Where children are on a part-time (out of school) timetable their attendance will be affected. The sessions where they are not in school must be recorded as absences, albeit authorised ones. The school may forget and send warning notices about attendance (it's an automated system), but as you will have the part-time timetable as an agreement in writing then this should be easily rectified. Additional absences are tempting with a part-time timetable. I recall many students who 'skived' a few half days as they just couldn't be bothered to come in. This will also be recorded as an absence and in this case unauthorised.

Part-time timetables should only ever be short-term measures, ideally reviewed at a minimum of every 2 weeks with a view to increasing back to full-time as soon as possible. Changes are best made in small stages, building on success and not subject to achieving impossible goals.

Tom was excluded 2 days for persistent disruption in class. It was suggested that he returned on a part-time timetable. The timetable was constructed such that he attended for half days and accessed lessons in which he would be successful. A review period was set for each Friday afternoon with the aim of adding a new subjects or attendance over unstructured breaks each week. By the end of the 4th week, Tom would be back on a full-time timetable.

Nell was also excluded for persistent disruption. She had a timetable constructed which required her to attend 3 hours each morning. The review period was set for 3 weeks. Nell was working hard and looking forward to having her timetable increased to include lunchtimes. The school refused and said they'd reconsider after another review period. Nell had to leave before lunch and half-way through a lesson. The review period was set for a further 3 weeks. Nell began to slip into her old behaviours. After 12 weeks she was still only attending 3 hours each morning.

60% of parents offered a part-time timetable didn't realise they could say no and also found that the timetable was not reviewed, often with their child remaining part-time for the remainder of the year.

Managed Moves

I've been involved with managed moves for many years through something called the fair access panel. This panel meets to assign students with no school place to a suitable school. Very often, when students have been permanently excluded trying to find their next school can be tricky and the panel can help find the most appropriate (and hopefully, the most successful) school for them. Whilst many schools may have locally agreed arrangements for managed moves between them, the fair access panel provides access to additional establishments.

I am the chair of governors in a trust that never permanently excludes students. We operate several primary and secondary schools, have two special schools and our own alternative provisions. Where a student ought to be permanently excluded, we have the option of placing them into another school within the trust. Where a placement within the trust is an issue, we have local school agreements with a number of schools in the area. Should none of these be suitable or accepted by the family then we can take to the fair access panel for access to a wider range of possibilities. As a result of our membership on the panel it means that we often take in new students who would otherwise have been permanently excluded from their own schools.

Managed moves work best where everyone has the full set of facts and take the opportunity for a fresh start. Whilst the child is on their trial period at the host school they remain on their own school's register. Their placement is reviewed regularly with a view to them transferring to the host school's register after the trial period (which is usually 6 weeks, although can be extended if necessary.)

Not every school operates the same way, but our process is as follows:

1. Child is at risk of permanent exclusion. A meeting is called with the family to discuss a managed move. Suitable alternative schools are discussed.

2. We approach the schools and ask if they will take the student. All information is shared with them. No cover up! This will include their academic profile, any SEN information and a brief overview of the family dynamics and any safeguarding concerns.

3. The host school agrees to take them on a half-term trial (if moving part way through the term, it will be for the remainder of this half term plus one full half term following.)

4. As their home school we arrange a new uniform (yes, we pay) and if transport costs are involved, we pay these for the duration of the trial. We take the child and their parents to visit the school and agree a start date. Where the child in in Key Stage 4, options are considered. A copy of any relevant files or information are transferred to the host school.

5. Depending on the needs of the student we might attend the school with them, dipping in over the first week, so that not everything is new, and they don't feel abandoned. For other students it is better to 'cut off' ties as quickly as possible. A review date at the end of week 2 will look at how things are going. Any incidents or problems are reported to the home school and the parents at the same time. If the student is involved in any incidents the host school can issue sanctions as appropriate to their school (detentions etc), but exclusions can only be issued by the home school. The host school can terminate the agreement at any point.

6. At each review (we attend every 2 weeks) progress and behaviour are considered. Children whose placement looks like it will break down, or not be successful will be fully informed and the home school will be looking for any alternatives. The host school will treat the child as one of their own.

7. At the final review meeting, the host school takes the child onto their school role and all normal transfer processes happen. There should be no ugly surprises at the review meeting.

Very rarely, we extend the managed move, perhaps because a student has had a prolonged absence and not been able to demonstrate their potential or there has been an incident in the last few days which is causing concern.

99% of our managed moves are successful because of the supportive processes we put in place. In schools I have previously worked in the success rate was around 65%.

As the host school it is important to handle the student as 'one of the school' and not make them out to be on a trial period or different to anyone else transferring mid-year.

Why do managed moves fail?

- The home school is not entirely honest with the host school.
- The student and/or their family don't really want the new placement.

- The home school does not provide support to the host school or pupil.
- The school chosen is not suitable for the child's needs.
- The triggering incident involved gang culture and students from the host school.
- The host school don't really want them and have been cornered. (It happens!)

When a managed move fails the home school takes the child back onto their own role. They cannot then issue a permanent exclusion for the original offence; however, they can look at placement in another school or alternative provision rather than take the child back into the school.

Pupil Referral Unit

PRUs are Pupil Referral Units. They are generally run by local authorities as their provision for excluded pupils. However, some PRUs offer outreach placements (at a cost) to their local schools. Where a child is at risk of permanent exclusion, they can be sent to the PRU for a fixed period of time. These placements are designed to be supportive. Perhaps, where a child is exhibiting a specific set of needs and further assessment is required. As schools pay for these placements, they are usually short-term (6-12 weeks) and can even be part-time placements with the other part of the time in their home school.

I've worked with a very successful PRU in the past who took students on 6-week placements in order to conduct assessments and provide behaviour management programs. With class sizes of 2 staff to 6-7 students in each class and a flexibility around uniforms and soft starts they were often able to unpick the needs of the students very well. Their program then involved a transition back to their own school over a further period of 6 weeks. Part of the week in the PRU and part in their home school with a member of staff from the PRU supporting and providing training and advice to the home school.

The expertise in PRUs is wide and when used well these placements can be highly successful. Unfortunately, with the increase in permanent exclusions and a crisis in appropriate availability in special schools, many PRUs find themselves stretched and unable to offer their outreach services so these are sadly on the decline.

When it doesn't work:

- Placing a Y6 child in a PRU for the final term. This does not help with transition to secondary nor with 'closing' at primary school and often means they miss out on things like the school camp.

- Where the child is highly susceptible, shy or copies the behaviour of those around them. PRUs are for the most extreme behaviours and include the children who have been permanently excluded. Whilst not exactly a hot bed of criminality, they can be challenging places to be.

- Where the child is unable to travel for distances. Each local authority generally has just one or two PRUs, meaning that a degree of travelling is required.

- Where the school is paying for the placement as an alternative provision with no intention of ever integrating the child back into their own school. I once transitioned a young man to secondary school whose primary school had paid for his place in a PRU since the first term of Year 4. Needless to say, transitioning from 2 staff and 6 students to a secondary school with 1 teacher to a class of 30 (and a TA only in core lessons) he did not do so particularly successfully and was permanently excluded before the summer term of Y7.-

Alternative Provision

AP is also the commonly used abbreviation for Alternative Provision. It is an education but not in a school. They are usually found in off-site locations, although some schools are involved in running their own APs. School run APs are inspected as part of the school whereas those run independently are inspected by OFSTED separately. An AP must be registered if it offers more than 6 hours education a week. There are criteria around fire regulations, health and safety and safeguarding which must be met. In my own local authority, only approved providers can be used, so not only do the APs have to meet OFSTED criteria they need to meet those of the local authority too.

Some Alternative Provisions are better than others and in some local authorities the availability is so dire that 100% of the APs have been graded as inadequate by OFSTED.

Whilst a student is attending an alternative provision, they are still on role at their home school. This means the home school is responsible for ensuring the quality of the education provided by the AP.

With a part-time timetable or a managed move, the parents have to agree to the placement. With an AP placement, parental consent as such is not required. If the offer of an AP is declined by the family, then the child is likely to be permanently excluded instead.

There are two uses of an AP.

The first use is as a short-term placement with the idea of improving the behaviours seen in school. This placement can be full- or part-time and is similar to the paid placement with a PRU. These shorter-term placements do not tend to have an academic focus and therefore have to be supplemented with a school education, tutors or additional AP at a more academic site. For example, in my area we have a fishing provision, where children are taken for 2-days a week to go fishing. The programme is designed to give support to the development of young people's self-esteem, confidence and achievement.

The second use is a longer-term placement usually at Key Stage 4 as an alternative or additional to attending school. These placements can be full- or part-time again. With older students the APs tend to offer qualifications although not all will offer a full GCSE package. Many courses are vocational in nature, things like mechanics or hair & beauty. It would be fair to say that they are of variable quality. Some APs operate like an extended work experience providing students with a taste of the adult world alongside their traditional qualifications.

Schools cannot access these provisions for free. They are generally quite expensive and there may be a quota on how many places a school can 'buy', not just from their own budgetary constraints but also from the provider themselves who don't want a full class of students from school X making up their cohort. The availability for younger children is more limited.

When it works:

- With Key Stage 4 pupils who have disengaged from traditional education, a package of AP and school provided curriculum can provide a suitable alternative.
- Where the AP holds a specific interest to the student.
- Where communication between the AP and the school is clear and regular.

Internal

A school may determine that a child's behaviour should result in a fixed-term exclusion, however they recognise that this can cause serious repercussions for the family as a whole. In this situation, they may decide to use an internal exclusion. It is not marked as an exclusion on a child's record as they are still attending school, provided with school work and often taught in small groups, but away from their usual classes.

There is a world of difference between these internal exclusions and 'isolation booths', although both may be used.

An internal exclusion is an exclusion served in school for a fixed period of time as an alternative to being sent home. It might involve sitting in the office of a member of staff, attending a special group of students who are also excluded from their main classes, or even sitting at a desk in a corridor outside the headteacher's office. It might also be served in a sanction room used in school for students who are sent out of lessons, and where 'booths' are provided to stop students communicating with each other.

I always read with interest about students who have spent a week in 'isolation'. Digging deeper, they should probably have been excluded for 5-days, but the school has accommodated them (perhaps so that parents can continue to work). Unfortunately, some students do not appreciate this and therefore misbehave in the provision, resulting in a further period of 'exclusion' being issued. It is easy to see how some students could end up spending a period of time in the booths.

Having spent most of my career working with children who have special educational needs, they are ironically the ones who quite like the isolation rooms and booths. Smaller classes, a quiet controlled environment, staff on hand to support and a structured routine. I have had many a student over the years deliberately mess about on entering a lesson they dislike in order to get sent out!

Where this doesn't work:

- Where it's seen as a better alternative to going to lessons
- Where it is poorly managed, lacks rules and becomes a 'fun' environment
- Where the behaviour of students is not challenged
- Where students do not understand that it is an alternative to something more serious

Pastoral Support Plan

A pastoral support plan or behaviour support plan is not going to solve any problems, but it does generate a clear idea of what everyone is working towards. All of the above alternatives should ideally be supported with a plan of some description which has clear short-term goals, an identified mentor and a defined review period. Children exhibit behaviour as a sign of unmet need and unless counselling or behaviour support is also provided as an element of the plan then any changes are unlikely.

Every school has its own way of creating behaviour support plans. In some schools they take the format of a home-school agreement or a report whereas in others they may resemble an individual education plan. What they look like is less important than the message they convey or the audience that reads them.

Secondary schools, by their very nature, are larger and have more staff involved with individual pupils than they would normally meet in a primary school. Whereas a primary school behaviour plan might be an agreement with the class teacher about a number of targets to achieve and an agreed classroom approach, in a secondary school it is one or two people agreeing on behalf of all of the staff what will be put into place and the goals to meet.

Without making excuses for secondary schools, this is difficult. We are not robots and just as our children have different personalities so do our staff. I'm sure you recall the teachers you got on with better at school and it wasn't necessarily because you enjoyed their subject. Our subjects lend themselves to different approaches. Often it is not the lack of communication in a secondary school that leads to a behaviour plan 'failing' but the natural variation in application.

The best behaviour plans allow for some flexibility for the benefit of the student and the staff involved.

Transfer

As an almost last resort, children could opt for a transfer to another school. This usually happens when the family has lost all faith in the current school. However, it would be unlawful for any school to suggest you transfer to another establishment to avoid an exclusion. Where relationships within the school are strained, perhaps with peer groups or on public transport to and from school, the family might want to explore alternatives. This is normally something that has been in the pipeline for a while before any fixed-term or permanent exclusions arise to the surface.

The advantage of a transfer is a fresh start without the need for a trial period to be passed. The disadvantage is that your child is starting from scratch without the previous school providing support and guidance other than a file of information once they've started which may not convey the message correctly.

The home school should NEVER make this suggestion to you. That would be unlawful and is often cited in examples of illegal off-rolling. If you want to move your child to another school, that is your choice – but you should NEVER feel pressured into moving your child to avoid an exclusion.

Transfers do not come with the buffer offered with a managed move and they do not have the same pre-movement sharing of information.

School Procedure...

I think it always comes as a shock to those outside of the education system just how much bureaucracy is involved in everyday decisions. Three quotes to buy a pack of toilet rolls, 2 full pages of documentation to complete to buy a pack of pencils. With this in mind, it is of no surprise that issuing an exclusion is fraught with paperwork and officialdom.

Caught up in the moment, you may feel that the school has made a knee-jerk decision, however this is very unlikely considering the number of hoops they will have had to jump through to conclude that they are issuing an exclusion.

As soon as a school becomes aware of issues, for example a student not following classroom instructions, they move to put measures in place to stop things escalating further. It might include issuing short, sharp sanctions, putting the child on report or referring to the school SENCO. It is rare that a child ends up with an exclusion without there being some warning signs first.

Of course, an argument in the playground or community that spills over into a full-fist-fight would be an exception to this.

Before making the decision to exclude a school has to take a number of things into consideration: the balance of probabilities, their duty of care, alternative solutions and ultimately what is best for everyone concerned.

The balance of proof

I always stifle a smile when I read Facebook comments along the lines of 'that school is a law unto themselves' or 'they think they are the judge and jury'. All decisions made by a school are made in line with administrative law. This includes exclusions.

There are 5 key words: **LAWFUL**

RATIONAL

REASONABLE

FAIR

PROPORTIONATE

This means that every decision (including exclusions) must consider the above. When asked as a governing body to review permanent exclusions these are the underpinning factors, we have to apply around the headteacher's decision.

A school is only required to apply the **CIVIL** standard of proof when looking at evidence.

> "On the balance of probabilities,
> it is more likely than not that this fact is true..."

This is different to the **CRIMINAL** standard which says "beyond reasonable doubt..."

What did I tell you about bringing woodworking tools into computing labs?!

On the balance of probabilities this child just smashed the computer screen.

It is the first lesson of the day and the classroom has brand new furniture. Tom (known for his graffiti around the community) is sat at a desk with a large black marker pen in his hand and there are obscene drawings on the table.

On the balance of probabilities, it is more likely than not that Tom drew on the desk.

However, it is not beyond reasonable doubt!

The headteacher lawfully excludes Tom for vandalism.

It doesn't end there though. Tom's headteacher has to consider whether the decision they have made is lawful, rational, reasonable, fair and proportionate.

	No	Yes
Is it lawful?	The headteacher excludes Tom for 5 days, but because they were unable to remove the marker pen from the tables, he converts the exclusion to a permanent one.	The headteacher excludes Tom for 5 days citing vandalism as the reason.
Is it rational?	The headteacher decides that Tom must also be responsible for all graffiti in the school and therefore adds this on to his exclusion. There is no evidence that Tom had access to the areas with the graffiti.	The headteacher finds graffiti on the chair at Tom's desk. He is accused of this as well.
Is it reasonable?	The headteacher gives Tom a duster to clean the desk and issues a fixed-term exclusion when he fails to clear it all.	The caretaker uses chemicals to remove the graffiti and Tom has to wipe the desks down with soap and water.
Is it fair?	Tom and Nell both did the same thing. Tom gets a 5-day exclusion. Nell just gets told not to do it again.	Tom and Nell both did the same thing. Tom gets a 5-day exclusion, Nell gets a 3-day exclusion and spends 2 evening detentions cleaning desks.
Is it proportionate?	Tom is excluded and sent a bill for the one piece of graffiti on his desk. He is not allowed to sit at or on any of the new furniture for the remainder of the academic year.	Tom is asked to contribute towards the replacement of the desk (as the graffiti could not be removed.)

Nothing is cut and dried, and even the examples above could be reversed depending on the other information available.

Duty of care

When you send your child into school, we take over their care for the day. A school still has a duty of care when sending a child home for an exclusion. Under normal circumstances they will contact the home and a parent will be asked to collect the child. Rarely, when the parent is unable to do so, they child may be asked to leave the school site to go to a safe location (make their own way home, grandparents, neighbour etc). This is usually only done following a conversation with the family. If your child usually makes their own way to and from school then this would not be unreasonable, they are only doing what they would normally do, albeit at a different time of the day. The school is likely to check that they have the key to get in the house and usually ask for them to make contact once they arrive. If the school is aware of issues that could make things difficult for the child at home (for example they are aware of housing problems, living in a hostel, or domestic abuse) then they should try to avoid exclusions and make alternative arrangements.

Children who travel with their family to and from school for SEN purposes (i.e. they are not safe crossing the road on their own), shouldn't be allowed to leave the school site. However, even this isn't as simple as it sounds. If a pupil leaves the school site, then staff at the school are required to inform the parents and the police, they then usually (if staffing allows) follow at a safe distance and we would expect them to intervene if the child is being abducted or runs into the middle of a busy road. But, as children in a state of anxiety can do unpredictable things, they often will not 'drag' them back into school or approach them for fear of them running off where they cannot be found or reaching an even higher state of anxiety. This can be murky waters for schools between the parent who expects their child to be dragged back into school kicking and screaming and physically manhandled, to the one who states that staff cannot 'handle' (touch) their child. As a parent, who has had a child try to run in front of a car, I can tell you that grabbing hold of one arm and pulling them backwards is likely to leave a mark, whoever does it! The alternative is a squashed child. Whilst positive handling doesn't hurt a child, in an emergency what would you, honestly, want someone to do?

The letter

There are sample letters included in the appendix that a school might send following an exclusion. There will be local variations, but the content should be similar.

The official letter should be sent promptly (without delay), and in the majority of circumstances it is handed over with the child at the point of exclusion.

The letter must include:

- Length of the exclusion if fixed term, or clearly state that it is a permanent exclusion

- Reason for the exclusion (it may be written out, but it should be clearly identifiable as one of the reasons from the school policy or the table presented in the section 'what can they exclude for'.

- When to return to the school (if fixed-term)

- The right to represent at a meeting of the governors (if the exclusion is 5+ days, or has accumulated more than 5 days)

- Who to contact/how to challenge

- How to obtain a set of your child's records

- Arrangements for education if the exclusion is longer than 5 days, including any reference to alternative provision. For shorter exclusions it may just state how the work is to be accessed for that time period.

- The parental responsibility around public spaces

An Education

Every child, no matter the length of the exclusion, should be provided with appropriate work to complete. This includes a half day exclusion, although the chances are at primary school it will be an instruction to read their book.

Where the exclusion is up to 5 days in length then the school or academy is responsible for providing the work. Often it is not given the same day as the exclusion occurs as school's need to go to the teaching staff and collate appropriate materials. Generally, it is submitted as a work pack, although some schools will set online activities to be completed. If you do not have access to online facilities make sure the school is aware of this and has the opportunity to provide something different. If your child usually receives support in school, then they may not be able to do the sent work without your assistance, although the work should be pitched at their level. (For example; an appropriate level of maths work to your child's ability, but they are unable to read the questions, so you may need to support.) The work set does not usually take them a full school day to complete. Children working 1:1 or on their own without distractions, registers, or 'teaching input' tend to complete work much faster.

From the 6th day of an exclusion (including permanent and longer fixed-term exclusions) the school, academy or local authority needs to arrange a suitable full-time education. With permanent exclusions the responsibility lies with the home local authority. For fixed-term exclusions the responsibility lies with the school or academy. We know, from research, that this does not always happen. Sometimes, it is because the family is opposing the exclusion and therefore refusing the PRU placement or they just don't want their child to attend what is offered.

Children permanently excluded in Key Stage 4, rarely make it in to a new school. Unfortunately, this has a major impact on their lifetime achievements. In 2008, less than 1%

of pupils in PRUs achieved 5x A*-C in their GCSES and only 11.7% achieved 1x A*-C. Whilst PRUs are supposed to be short-term it is becoming more common for them to be named on an EHCP for Key Stage 2 and 3 and to hear stories of children in there for several years.

(Note: the GCSE examinations grading system recently changed, and grades are now issued from 9 to 1 rather than A* to G. The old good passes of A*-C are now represented by grades 4 and above.)

Comparatively for children attending Alternative Provisions only 6% achieve the 5 good GCSEs, and 80% of all children classed as excluded at the end of their secondary provision will not be in Education, Employment or Training (NEET) the following year.

The school or local council must tell you about any alternative education they arrange, but it's your responsibility to make sure your child attends. If alternative education isn't arranged within 5 days, or you're not happy with the education, you can complain to:

- the school, for fixed period exclusions
- the local council, for permanent exclusions

If you're not happy with the response, you can complain to the Department for Education (DfE), and you'll need to show that you followed the school or council's complaints procedure.

Dealing with the school roll

When a student is no longer a member of a school then the headteacher has a duty to remove them from their roll.

If only life were so simple.

What happens in reality is that they cannot be removed from the role until the sequence of governors' meetings and appeals is completed.

If a family decides not to contest or appeal the exclusion and simply wants to move on, then you can inform the school of this and they can start the process much quicker, allowing you to register your child at a new establishment.

On the other hand, if you attend the governors' meeting, appeal to an Independent Review Panel and then take this further to a judicial review you could be looking at your child's name remaining on the school register for upwards of 5 months.

The responsibility for removing the child from the role lies with the headteacher of their school.

School must tell

When a student is excluded the school is required to inform the parents immediately, but they also have a duty to inform a number of other bodies too.

For permanent exclusions, they need to inform their governing body and the representative individual at the local authority immediately. This is so that the governing body can convene their meeting before the 15 days deadline and so that the local authority can organise alternative education from day 6 of the exclusion. There is nothing stopping a parent from also informing the Director of Children's Services at the local authority of the exclusion and reminding them of their duty to arrange provision.

With fixed term exclusions of more than 5 days or 10 lunches the school must, again, inform the governing body, the local authority and where relevant their trust immediately. In the case of an academy, they are required to organise a suitable education from day 6 whereas for a maintained school this falls to the local authority. These are not cumulative exclusions, so 3 2-day exclusions will not trigger this. However, where the number of exclusions exceeds 15-days in one term (Autumn, Spring or Summer) then the governing body must hold a meeting with the family invited. This meeting is run on the same basis as a permanent exclusion and is a clear indication that your child is at risk of permanent exclusion from the school.

For exclusions of less than 5 days the local authority 'exclusions return' only needs to be sent on a termly basis.

Where a child has an EHCP, their permanent exclusion must be flagged to their local authority immediately, although there is no such requirement for fixed-term exclusions, therefore parents might like to inform their case worker themselves.

Children who are looked after have a second headteacher called the virtual head who must also be informed immediately of any fixed-term or permanent exclusions.

Governors of schools (maintained and academies) tend to hold full board meetings at least three times a year. These meetings include a section called the 'headteacher's report' where they are required to update the governing body on any exclusions in the previous term. These updates are not detailed and simply involve passing on the number of students involved, the year groups and the duration of each exclusion. Governors challenge schools with what they are doing to ensure smooth reintegration, reduce the exclusions or what early intervention is in place.

Penalties and fines

Long gone are the days where excluding students had no impact on schools. For many years now the funding allocated to that student (called the AWPU – average weighted pupil unit) has been made to follow a permanently excluded student. This is recouped by the local authority from the school and might be passed on to their next establishment or the PRU. This proves an interesting situation for secondary schools. They are 'lag funded'. In other words, when a student starts in Y7 their presence on the school role is not acknowledged until the census in October. It then takes until the following April before any funding or money follows them. If a Y7 student is excluded before the April then the school won't have received any money for them, nor will they receive the funding, yet they will have had their AWPU reclaimed by the local authority.

Schools can also be fined by the independent review panel (IRP) if they decide not to reinstate a pupil within 10 days of the IRP suggesting that they should. This fine is £4000.

At one point a few years ago, some local authorities also moved to a system whereby you got a limited number of 'free' exclusions each year and then had to pay a fine relative to the number of years remaining on role (therefore a Y7 cost 5x the amount of excluding a Y11).

Whilst many will see this as an incentive designed to get schools to retain pupils on role, in reality all it did was reduce the amount of funding available to support those students and others to remain in the school.

Reintegration

Reintegration is the most important element of an exclusion. How a school (and family) handle this will determine the child's future success.

The reintegration meeting is not compulsory, and some schools simply issue the exclusion, it is served, and the child arrives back in class at the end without any further address. These are the least successful uses of an exclusion.

A good reintegration meeting will have the parents, child and school meeting together to discuss the events that led up to the exclusion and building a plan to ensure it doesn't happen again. For some students, especially those on the autistic spectrum, this can be difficult, but it should not be ignored. This meeting can be used to clear the air, demonstrate that the exclusion is now in the past and we need to move forward, and to establish what needs to happen next. For students with special educational needs it is important that the SENCO is involved in this meeting in order to look at the support and provisions already in place and suggest changes or additional work that can be down.

From the reintegration meeting, a clear plan should be generated. Many secondary schools will have a child on 'report' for a short period after an exclusion usually with 2-3 achievable targets generally related to the reason for the exclusion – for example: to sit where the teacher directs, to complete classwork, to have all their equipment. It is important to note that failure to meet these report targets should not automatically result in a further exclusion although they often lead to an extension in the time 'on report'.

A pastoral support plan or behaviour plan might be proposed from the reintegration meeting. This document, similar to the individual education plans often used for special educational needs, identifies the desired behaviours and ways to achieve them. Unlike a STAR or ABC analysis they are not for analysis behaviours but more for putting the measures in place to reduce anything undesirable. Students with autistic spectrum difficulties can find a 5-point scale useful in communicating their feelings and likely behaviours.

Incident procedure

Following any incident in school there is usually a process or procedure that comes in to play. Whether that is formalised or whether it is an individual's 'normal way' of actioning things is a decision for the school.

In a primary school, it is common for the headteacher or another member of the SLT to deal with a serious incident from the outset. They are likely to be involved in collecting the pupil statement, investigating the incident and then making the decisions/recommendations.

In secondary schools, it is more likely to be a member of the pastoral team who undertakes the work. This might be the head of year/house, a non-teaching inclusion lead or a mentor. These staff conduct all the required processes before taking their findings to their line manager who will decide whether it is to be taken to the headteacher for a possible exclusion.

At each step of the way there are likely to be records generated. From witness statements to pupil voice, CCTV footage or photos, and even medical records. If you choose to appeal the exclusion, then you should be given copies of these (although medical records may be transcribed and severely redacted if they are not directly related to your child.)

My personal procedure was as follows, bearing in mind I would usually be dealing with students who have just been involved in a fight:

1	Made aware of an incident involving one of my students. Arrange cover for any class I might be teaching.
2	Find the student and make sure that they are OK. Check if they need medical attention and organise. Provide a drink and biscuit if necessary.
3	Ask the student for a brief summary and who was a witness. If they are ready, ask them to write their statement. Even those who struggled with writing were asked to write their own statement and then we discussed and wrote their version together...the process of getting some points down on paper is very good at calming and focussing.
4	Organise for all witnesses to be collected and separated before stories could be created! Check each statement, reading back to the student and allowing them to provide extra detail/correct.
5	Discuss with my own student whether they had any other choices they could have made to avoid what had happened. This is useful in establishing whether they have remorse for what has just happened, but also in finding out if they understand why it happened and if they know how to avoid in the future.

6	Collate all the information and take to my line manager armed with the behaviour policy and any mitigating arguments. My aim was always to try and keep my students in school and avoid an exclusion or at least minimise it.
7	From the line managers decision, take to the headteacher who would have the final say on how long any exclusion would be for.
8	If the student was to be excluded, phone the family and make arrangements for them to come and collect their child as soon as feasible. Keep the student with me in my office (or at the back of my lessons).
9	Organise work for the student to take home with them. Speak with the office and complete the statutory paperwork. This would include calculating how many previous exclusions and locating current reading and spelling ages and their identified support in school.
10	Meet the family on arrival and explain the situation. Take their child over to meet them. Provide the letter of exclusion or explain I would drop it off on my way home later.
11	Arrange a reintegration meeting. We usually do this the morning that the child is due back in school, but, as I taught, we sometimes had to look at alternatives. If parents could not attend a reintegration meeting the child would still return to school but would have the meeting with me and without everyone else present.
12	Whilst the child is absent from school, look at the exclusion and what led up to it and create a plan to avoid further exclusions. This might form the basis of a PSP or BSP. As the students under my care would likely be on the SEN register, review support and provisions available and see if any changes can be made.
13	Email all relevant teaching staff to inform them of the planned absence, the requirement to provide work, and the planned return. After the reintegration meeting make sure staff are aware of any changes or adaptations and this may mean the child does not immediately return to lessons on that day.

Pupil voice

If you are accused of something, then you have the right to explain your side of the story. Ideally, this needs to be done whilst it is fresh in the mind, but adrenaline often makes it difficult for students to focus on this. As soon as possible, after any incident that is to result in an exclusion, a student should be given the opportunity to put forward their side.

We are not always aware of everything going on and perhaps the reason Tom didn't want to sit down and was running around the classroom, was because he had wet pants! We wouldn't know this unless we listened to him.

Children should be encouraged to write their version as a statement. This allows them to use their own words. Even young children and those with learning difficulties can use pen and paper to draw or write words/bullet points. These can then be used by an adult to help the child reconstruct their version of events.

Non-verbal children, without written skills, will find this very difficult. They can be asked to role play the events and use their preferred mechanism of communication. A series of emotion faces can be very useful for this.

Statements

Schools are required to look at that 'balance of probabilities' and taking statements from other individuals can be helpful here.

Any adults are often asked to give their version of what was observed, and children are asked to write their 'statement'. It is important that collusion is not allowed ("getting the story straight") and that all witnesses of the 'accused' are asked to contribute, even if they say they saw nothing.

These statements allow those who were not present to try and picture the event.

Whilst some schools provide a blank sheet of paper, others will give a writing framework to prompt students with their piece. Even those students with lower level writing skills can be encouraged to add bullet points, single words, diagrams and pictures in order to get across their version. From these an adult can mediate to turn the 'notes' into a 'statement'.

Date	Time	Name	Requested by
Date of incident	Time of incident	Who else was there?	Words & phrases you could use:
			I was...
			I saw...
What were you doing before the incident?			I felt...
			I heard...
			I had...
			Scared
			Shouted
What happened during the incident?			Screamed
			Pushed
			Hit
			Fight
			Threw
			Running around
			Crying
			Teacher
			Classroom
			Dinner lady
What happened after the incident?			

Example primary school writing frame for a statement.

Letters

You would be amazed how much a letter of apology can achieve.

Where a student has participated in a one-off offence which has resulted in a permanent exclusion a well written and heart-felt apology letter could be all it takes to have that decision overturned.

With shorter fixed-term exclusions, it is likely to have little impact, and for students who are on their third of fourth exclusion the phrase 'actions speak louder than words' is pertinent!

When a student assaults a member of staff it frequently ends in a permanent exclusion, unions are powerful bodies and no teacher or TA goes to work to be assaulted. A letter of apology may make the difference between that member of staff pursuing a police charge of assault or not. It can also make the school think twice about whether they will permanently exclude or issue a long fixed-term exclusion.

Always worth a try!

Parent Procedure

Once you are informed that your child has been excluded the chances are you will be thrown into a world of turmoil.

There are a number of steps that you need to take, some more obvious than others but included for clarities sake.

1	Make arrangements to collect your child, or for them to make their way home or to a safe place.
2	Ask the person giving you the information for as much detail as possible: Length of the exclusion Reason When you will be receiving the letter What work needs to be completed, and when/how it will be provided For exclusions longer than 5 days check the arrangements for alternative provision/education from day 6
3	Decide on your family arrangements for the length of the exclusion. Who will look after your excluded child? What arrangements are needed for other children in the family? Do you need to rearrange anything for yourself?
4	Make sure that you follow the exclusions guidance (in your letter) carefully, so as not to fall foul of any laws or generate any fines. Encourage your child to complete any work that has been set to the best of their ability.
	If you decide to challenge the exclusion or make a complaint you will need to ask for (or source on the website):
A	The behaviour and discipline policy of the school Complaints policy SEN policy (if relevant)
B	You will need to put in a formal request to the DPO (data protection Officer) for a SAR (Subject Access Request)
C	Request copies of the evidence and a report of the incident from the relevant person at the school (this is usually the person who delivered the news that your child is excluded.) Ask for the investigation records although be aware that any witness statements may be redacted.

Subject Access Request (SAR)

Your child's school file should contain up-to-date information about their academic achievement, any correspondence, attendance records, historical school reports, and in many cases a record of any previous incidents.

It is not uncommon for the file to contain a whole host of useless items too, such as copies of test papers from Year 2! When a child is placed on school report the copies of the report generally make their way into this long-term storage.

A Subject Access Request is the method used to obtain a copy of your child's file.

So, why do you need this?

Well, most of you might already have and if you are a wonderfully organised individual the chances are it might all be stored in chronological order in a ring binder for easy access somewhere in your house. I can make a general bet, that the rest of us, might still have it, in a drawer, folder, box somewhere and child number 1 might have their things mixed up with child 2. I can also guess that if you've moved to a new house at any point you probably can't find any of them although you're sure you saw it last week! Some of us might even admit to having binned them in a massive clear-out at some point.

This file and its contents are useful if you want to show any patterns of behaviour or demonstrate that your child's needs have not been met.

The school will have a named Data Protection Officer and it is best to make your request directly to this person. Personally, I recommend email as you have a time-stamped trail.

You don't need everything from the file and if you are specific then the school is less likely to be awkward or drag the request out to the last minute. There are statutory guidelines around the time-scale they have to reply, which for a simple request is 28 days. Unlike the old 'copy of school file' request, schools are no longer allowed to charge for the time to create this file nor the photocopying. Be aware of this, since the message seems not to have filtered through to all of them who are operating on old timescales and processes. (I even had to correct one of my own schools recently who informed me they would refuse a request as it takes them too long to action and the £10 fee, they charge isn't enough to cover their time!)

Some of the contents of the file will have thick black lines through them. This is redaction and serves to remove the information of other identifiable individuals; usually names. If your child has ever reported a safeguarding concern, or school have recorded their concerns, then this is not likely to make it into your SAR pack, even if you ask for everything. The information in a child's safeguarding file is confidential and protected. The only individual's in school with access are those designated as the school safeguarding leads (DSL) and it is rarely shared outside of this circle. The exceptions being, social care for an active case, the police (who usually come with a warrant or a request for a specific piece of information or time line) and under direction of a court order.

If your child is older than 13 then the school may ask for them to make the request rather than you being able to ask for it on their behalf.

Complaints

If you feel that things have not been dealt with correctly you can make a complaint. This is separate from appealing the exclusion (see the chapter on appeals.)

Very often when things are not going well, and we want to complain, we seem to think that jumping straight to the top will get us the result we want. Unfortunately, education doesn't work like that. If you attempt to go straight to the local authority or OFSTED, all that happens is that they forward your letter on to the school to see if they have had a chance to deal with it already. Where the answer is no, OFSTED and the LA, step back and leave it to the school. Families become frustrated since they feel that these bodies have ignored their request. Where the answer is yes, they will ask the school what has been done and 99/100 will make a note on the file to say that the school has taken appropriate action. Again, they don't usually inform the families of this!

Every school has a complaints procedure and if you want to get a result from your complaint then you need to follow this procedure closely. Schools that belong to an academy may have their complaints procedure hidden away on the website for the multi-academy trust, but if you can't find it, simply ask for a paper copy from the school reception.

The guidance a school is recommended to follow can be found on the DfE website: https://www.gov.uk/government/publications/school-complaints-procedures/best-practice-advice-for-school-complaints-procedures-2019 This is however, guidance and schools/academies can chose not to follow what is in it.

The complaints process of a school usually involves a putting it in writing to the headteacher of the school, if the response is not satisfactory (or is about the headteacher), then you write a letter of complaint to the governors. Do not assume that this is the chair of governors. I am the chair of governors in three schools and I do not deal with letters of complaint in any of them. I have a designated governor in each who does this – if you are not happy with their response it is escalated to me. If you are not happy with the response from the governors then you complain to the DfE (for a maintained school) or the ESFA (for an academy school), or if it relates to the manner in which a school is run then you complain to OFSTED.

Complaints have a limited life-span usually considered to be 3 months from the date of the thing you are complaining about.

Complaints about actual exclusions have their own process (the appeal) but if your complaint is about the behaviour policy then it must be done through the normal complaints procedure.

Challenging exclusion

(See section on Appeals)

You may disagree with the exclusion that has been issued. In this case you have to follow a different complaints process. It is entirely possible that you may have to challenge the exclusion and make a complaint about (for example) the behaviour policy at the same time.

The instructions for challenging an exclusion are included in the letter from the school telling you about the exclusion. A sample letter is in the appendix.

You can ask the school's governing body to overturn the exclusion (challenge the exclusion) If either:

- your child has been excluded for more than 5 days
- the exclusion means they'll miss a public exam or national curriculum test

If the exclusion is for 5 days or fewer, you can still ask the governors to hear your views, but they can't overturn the headteacher's decision.
In most cases by the time the meeting has been convened you child will have already served the exclusion. If this is the case, and the governors uphold your complaint, then a note will be put on your child's file, but the codes cannot be changed.
Permanent exclusions are challenged by default. There is an automatic review meeting with the school's governors if your child has been permanently excluded. This will happen within 15 school days. If the governors don't overturn the exclusion, you can ask for an independent review by your local council (or academy trust if the school's an academy). The governors must tell you how to do this.

If your child is still excluded you can ask the Local Government Ombudsman (or the Education Funding Agency if the school's an academy or free school) to look at whether your case was handled properly. They can't overturn the exclusion.

You can make a claim to a court or a tribunal if you think your child's been discriminated against. You need to do this within 6 months of the exclusion. The Equality Advisory Support Service is able to provide help and advice.

Vulnerable Groups

Children excluded at age 12 are 4x more likely to be in prison at age 24.

Some groups of students seem to receive more exclusions than others. Schools have to be careful they are not discriminating against those students.

It doesn't surprise me that SEND accounts for about 50% of all permanent exclusions. After all, if a student is displaying challenging behaviour in school, we are encouraged to add them to our SEN registers and to put measures or support in place, but sometimes things escalate too quickly or are beyond the remit or control of the school – hence they end up with exclusions. Quite honestly, I question how 50% of children not on the SEN register are being permanently excluded rather than the other way around. Children with SEND are 7x more likely to be excluded and 50% of those who are will have some recognised mental health issue.

If a decision to exclude would breach the Equality Act 2010, either because it was discriminatory or because reasonable adjustments had not been put in place prior to the exclusion, then an Independent Review Panel is likely to find that any decision of the governing body should be quashed.

If an Individual Review Panel finds that discrimination is in existence, then the parents can make a claim to the First Tier Tribunal within 6 months of the alleged discriminatory act.

A governing body needs to be satisfied that reasonable adjustments have been put in place for a pupil in the lead up to an exclusion. Where this is satisfied then they are not discriminating against a pupil with SEN if they decide to exclude.

E.g. if support should be in place but isn't because the TA is absent that day and no alternative arrangements have been put in place, then should the child be involved in a violent act as a result of their SEN a governing body could not justifiably uphold a decision to exclude.

If, however, the school had made an attempt to put a different TA in place, then they have made a reasonable adjustment and tried to meet the needs of the student in an appropriate manner. Any violent act resulting in an exclusion could be upheld by the body.

It is important to note that the requirement is to apply 'reasonable adjustments' and not '**all** possible adjustments'.

In August 2018, there was a landmark case where a young child with autism had been excluded from school following an act of violence. It was upheld that this was a manifestation of his meltdown and therefore an element of his disability for which they could not be discriminated against. In this particular case, there had been no reasonable adjustments in place to accommodate the disability.

It is essential to look beyond the behaviour and provide adequate support before seeking punitive measures.

Other groups which seem to be disproportionately represented in exclusion figures include those of Gypsy/Roma Heritage (Travellers), students of black Caribbean ethnicity, those who claim free school meals or who are looked-after.

Children who are looked-after (by the local authority in children's homes, fostered or even adopted) have often experienced adverse childhood experiences. They are 2x more likely to be permanently excluded. The human brain is highly formative during the first few years of development, and although they may not remember the circumstances around their removal to care, the experience will have imprinted and had an impact on their neurodevelopment. We know that that human body prioritises the survival instincts when under pressure and reinforces our primal instincts. Imagine our typical cave man, his priority was not on learning the alphabet or what a fronted adverbial is – more, he was concerned with finding his next meal and making sure he was not the next meal for some other predator. These primal instincts remain with us today, but most of us develop to rationalise and control our reactions. Wherever possible schools are expected to avoid excluding looked-after children and instead offer additional support or transfer to an alternative school. If your child is looked-after and facing exclusion, then make sure you are communicating with the Designated Teacher for Looked-After Children within the school and the Virtual Head who will be based at the local authority. Schools receive a small amount of additional funding (currently £2300) for LAC and post-LAC children which can be put towards ensuring support is provided.

Children who fall short of the looked-after category but who are classed as children in need because of safeguarding issues (for example, neglect, abuse or exposure to domestic violence) are not afforded the same protection or funding yet are 3x more likely to be permanently excluded. One has to wonder what we are exposing these children to by excluding them from the relatively safe, secure and stable environment of their school.

Children who receive free school meals are often over-represented in exclusion statistics, with up to 4x as many being excluded. The implication is that they live in communities of high deprivation where unemployment is high, gang culture is common and that the need to claim free school meals suggests that wider experiences and support at home are not available. Whilst this is a massive over generalisation, there is increasing evidence of childhood poverty and this brings us back to our primal instincts and need to survive. Children going home to cold houses and relying on foodbanks, wearing a pair of shoes too small or trousers that are grubby and ripped are disadvantaged. Children can be nasty creatures (!) and will spot the subtle things to 'pick on' other children for. This often escalates to bullying if not dealt with promptly. Whilst the bullying doesn't need to be physical or even verbal, simply isolating an individual from the 'in-crowd' can be enough to cause a rift. These children often retaliate quickly to any perceived criticism in order to protect their already fragile self-esteem. If the child has claimed free school meals (not universal free meals for infants) within the last 6 years, then the school receives additional money to try and address the differences between them and their peers. Called Pupil Premium, this money is currently worth £1320 for primary pupils and £935 for secondary. This is not a sum of money that must be spent on an individual, instead the money can be pooled to provide additional support. Many primary schools use the money to retain the general in-class support staff they would otherwise have lost, but with a remit to focus on pupil premium students. Others offer school uniform and contributions to school trips. One school, local to me, buys every child in the school a reading book every month, whereas another employs tutors, mentors and counsellors. Parents do not have any ability to demand how the money is spent, nor does the money have to be specifically spent on your child, but the school does have to demonstrate that their use of the funding has a positive impact on this vulnerable group.

Our black Caribbean and Gypsy/Roma or Irish Traveller children are also highly represented in exclusion figures. Not being from either of these communities it would not be appropriate for me to speculate on the reasons, However, I will summarise the work of others:

Children of the travelling community do not value education. For the girls it is seen as unnecessary and for the boys they will go to work in the family business as soon as they turn 13 or 14 years. Families do not support the educational structure and expectations. Students from these communities have poor attendance when they are in school resulting in difficulties keeping up with their peers. This in turn leads to disaffection in the classroom and misbehaviour. Social difficulties are evident with dysfunctional relationships with peers. They are 6 times more likely to be excluded a statistic which has varied little over the years.

Children, especially boys, of black Caribbean heritage are more vulnerable to exclusion, in fact if they have SEND and are free-school meals are 168 times more likely to be excluded than a female non-SEN, non-FSM child of white British heritage. Incidentally this group of students are also more likely to be identified under the old SEN system as having Behaviour/Emotional or Social Difficulties (1.5x more likely). Whereas the increased identification of hearing impairments in Bangladeshi students (2x) or multi-sensory impairments in Pakistani students (2x) is considered to be of genetic origin, there has been no proposed explanation for the increased identification of BESD in black Caribbean pupils although socio-economic factors (they are 2x more likely to come from a low income family) may come in to play. There is an indication that they are more likely to experience racism due to their distinctive appearance and in fact, the only explanation frequently cited for the reason behind the school exclusions suggests that the education system is inherently racist. With approximately 2% of the school population being black Caribbean and approximately 2% of teachers also fitting this descriptor (and about 2.5% of headteachers being anything other than white British) there is a proportionate representation amongst educational staff. Despite this, black Caribbean (and mixed white & black Caribbean) students account for 8% of all permanent exclusions. A figure 4x what we would expect it to be. The most interesting information stems from the fact that whilst black Caribbean (and mixed white & black Caribbean) children are more likely to be excluded the same does not hold true for black African or other children of black heritage. Other research suggests that the cultural behaviours and stereotypes lead to misunderstandings. In the West Indian culture children are expected to lower their eyes when being reprimanded, not look at the person, whereas in white British culture this is considered a sign of disrespect.

Our environment also throws in a few factors to complicate the situation. Childhood poverty (on the increase), adverse childhood experiences (ACEs), safeguarding concerns, longer working hours, parental and family conflict, housing and no doubt the preservatives or chemicals in our food will all impact on vulnerable youngsters.

> "Children of West Indian parents," declared an influential report in 1969, "the largest of all the immigrant groups, have been a source of bafflement, embarrassment and despair in the education system... They have often presented problems which the average teacher is not equipped to understand, let alone overcome."
>
> Over the 50 years since these words were written, there have been improvements in the lives and education of young British people of black Caribbean heritage. Attainment gaps have been closing slowly, and there is less "bafflement, embarrassment and despair." But young people of black Caribbean heritage, or of mixed black Caribbean and white heritage, are still many times more likely than others to be excluded, and there is still a widespread perception amongst parents and community leaders, that the causes lie in practices, routines and expectations in schools.

SEN

Behaviour is a communication.
Disruptive behaviour may be an indicator of unmet needs.

In the new SEN Code of Practice (September 2014) there was a shift from the use of Behaviour, Emotional and Social Difficulties (BESD) or Emotional Behavioural Difficulties (EBD) to Social, Emotional and Mental Health Difficulties (SEMH). The result of this was to encourage schools to look at the underlying causes of behaviour and identify the actual emotional, social or mental health need rather than blaming 'behaviour.

I began my teaching career when the only other adult in your classroom was a volunteer mum who stayed behind in the morning to listen to readers and change library books, or who popped in an hour early on a Thursday afternoon to wash the paint pots. The rest of the day we managed the children in our classrooms on our own. There were the pressures of performance tables and SATs along with OFSTED so this hasn't changed. However, the curriculum has changed dramatically. What I was teaching in Y8 maths when I began is now featured on the Y4 curriculum, and don't get me started on the literacy objectives which some university English professors admit to never having studied. Throw into the mix a child who struggles to learn in the first place and the demands of a curriculum which no longer revisits and reinforces information and we have a generation of frustrated youngsters who find it difficult to access lessons and therefore switch off or resort to what is perceived as disruptive behaviour.

I'm not blaming the rise of problems in the classroom entirely on the curriculum. There are environmental factors at play too. Children who were born extremely prematurely did not have the chance to fully develop their neural pathways. The primitive reflexes are prioritised as these are needed for survival. Some of these children present at school as 'immature', clumsy, 'behind' and 'needy'. They often react to their environment with extreme behaviours, without necessarily being aware of their actions.

We also have many children now attending school who present with foetal alcohol syndrome. Ten years ago, we would never have dared to suggest that mother's behaviour during pregnancy might be the cause of their child's learning or behaviour difficulties and often sought to find an alternative label. Foetal alcohol syndrome affects the neurodevelopment of the baby along with some physical characteristics. My education psychologist was fascinated by this field and once showed me pictures of a foetus developing. A drink of alcohol (one large glass of wine) on one date caused railroad track ears, on another date resulted in epicanthal folds (of the eyelids)…it wasn't so much that drinking during pregnancy caused issues, but that the formation of a human being inside the mother is so specific with its timeline that drinks on certain days affected very defined aspects which shocked me the most.

And then we address the special educational needs which most frequently present with behavioural facets. ADHD (Attention Deficit Hyperactivity Disorder) and ASC (Autistic Spectrum Difficulties/Condition). Both relatively recently 'labelled'. Those of us in our 40s will not have heard of these difficulties whilst we were at school. Officially ADHD was only recognised in the UK in 2000 (and 1980 in the US), whereas the modern definition of ASC in 1972, led to the condition being recognised in the UK from 1980 although most research has been conducted since 1985. Since the extreme forms of ASD (non-verbal, avoidant, repetitive behaviour and isolated) tended to be taught in special schools until 1997 when the Inclusion Policy introduced at that time suggested all children could and should be taught in mainstream schools. This led to widespread closures of special schools and the inclusion of all but the most extreme (usually wheelchair bound, unable to communicate or function independently) individuals with profound and multiple learning difficulties into regular primary and secondary classrooms. Thus, the profile of our schools changed but as is typical in education no one provided the training or support for teachers to assist those pupils and 20 years on we still have teacher training programs that skirt around the issue of special educational needs with the notion that staff will learn on the job.

Whilst very different difficulties, ADHD and ASC both present their behaviour challenges. From the impulsive and hyperactive behaviour of ADHD to the meltdowns and violent responses to sensory situations of ASC. (There has been a recent shift in language from ASD and Asperger's to the use of autism and ASC.)

Students with PDA (pathological demand avoidance) a more complex presentation of autism, often find themselves on the receiving end of an exclusion. A couple of the features of PDA include resistance to and avoidance of ordinary demands of life and using social strategies as a part of the avoidance. Phil Christie (NASEN March 2019) said 'The degree of adaptation and personalisation needed for many children with PDA doesn't sit easily alongside inflexible whole-school policies.'

Mental ill health in children is on the increase and can result in behaviour and conduct problems as well as emotional issues such as depression and anxiety.

Children who exhibit difficulties of a social, emotional or mental health manner, may well present with behaviour seen as challenging or anti-social. The language we recall from our childhood would be 'naughty', 'difficult', 'defiant' or 'troublesome'.

Negative behaviour is a way of communicating needs.

Children may have problems regulating their responses when they are stressed. The greater the stress the greater the chance of a child exhibiting a survival instinct: fight, flight or freeze.

It would be unusual to exclude or punish the child who hides under a table when stressed (or bursts into silent tears) but it is common to see a child who hits out when stressed excluded or punished.

Scared children do scary things. (Paul Clair. NASEN May 2018)

Anxiety in children can present as withdrawal and refusal to engage; lashing out in in the face of perceived threat; physical aggression or self-harm. Depression may present as low self-esteem resulting in low motivation, lack of engagement and rejection of help.

Statistically, 10% of children aged 5-16 have some form of mental health difficulty. Approximately, 5.8% of these have a conduct disorder, 3.7% an emotional disorder (such as anxiety or depression), 1-2% severe ADHD and 1% some other neurodevelopmental difficulty.

Historically, we were always taught to see the behaviour and the child as separate entities. We address naughty behaviour and not naughty children. However, recent studies suggest that the two should not be separated and instead we see the behaviour as an expression of the child's state of mind.

Teachers are often caught up in their teaching to the remainder of the class and may miss the subtle signs that things are going awry. ABC (Antecedent-Behaviour-Consequence) charts have been used for many years to analyse events and try to work out what happened and why before looking at alternative choices that could have been made. This assumes that the child is able to identify what happened before an event and is able to choose an alternative route or behaviour path. For other children the use of the Fantastic 5-Point Scale is often proposed. But again, if they are unable to identify and self-check how they are feeling at each part of the day, then they are not able to indicate where they are on the scale for others to help in avoiding the next stage.

With cuts to SEN budgets (and school budgets in general) and national increases in the costs of resources and salaries, it becomes less likely that classrooms have spare members of staff available to assist and the increasing demands from the curriculum are having an impact on students, staff and schools alike. In covert exclusions we considered that some children are regularly 'sent home' because their support is not available and 39% of classroom teachers do not know that this is an unlawful exclusion.

Balancing the needs of everyone

"A child with possible SEN (nothing confirmed) has been displaying increased behavioural outbursts over the last few weeks. It reached a head today when he pushed a pregnant staff member out of his way. The parents are livid that we have given him an internal exclusion for tomorrow. The teachers are livid that it is not an external exclusion."

Children with certain SEN are more likely to be excluded because of their nature. Most at risk are those with Autistic Spectrum Conditions, ADHD, Learning Difficulties or Social, Emotional and Mental Health needs. We know that the impact of their needs and the increased risk of exclusions can lead to much lower examination outcomes.

In 2017, 83.8% of a surveyed group of schools achieved 5 GCSES at grades A*-C. Only 72.4% of students labelled as ASC, 52.4% of those with ADHD, 68.9% of Learning Difficulties and 47.5% of SEMH children achieved the same. Knowing that attendance is also impacted on by exclusions (it's still an absence) the average for the group of schools was 94.5% and only 92.9% for those students with ASC. 9% of their ASC students had received exclusions of 6-10 days and 5% exclusions of more than 20 days.

In a longitudinal study, looking at children over a longer period of time, it was found that those students who had received a fixed term exclusion by age 8 were 15 times more likely to be excluded at age 16.

Children who have the highest level of needs are often granted an EHCP (education, health and care plan) which clearly directs the provision and support to be given in order to meet their needs. As a result of this legal framework there should not be a need to exclude these students, but where their behaviour reaches incineration point a school is obliged to do what it can to avoid a permanent exclusion wherever possible. The EHCP however won't 'shield' a child from exclusion where it is justified. If a child with an EHCP is permanently excluded, then the local authority has to convene an emergency review with haste since a new school will need to be consulted and named (unlike other students they can't just 'go to a PRU'.)

Equalities Act & Discrimination

The Equalities Act (2010) states that schools cannot discriminate against, harass or victimise children because of:

- Sex
- Race
- Disability
- Religion/belief
- Sexual orientation
- Pregnancy/maternity
- Or gender reassignment

This also made it incumbent upon schools to provide reasonable adjustments to policies and practices and the provision of auxiliary aids for disabled children. Reasonable adjustment does not mean every possible adjustment.

There is an additional duty called the Public Sector Equality Duty which means that in addition to the above, schools have to advance the opportunities of those with a protected characteristic and those who do not (often referred to as levelling the playing field) and foster relations between people who share protected characteristics and those who do not share it.

Until August 2018 there was a loophole which meant schools didn't need to make reasonable adjustments who had a tendency to physically abuse. However, this loophole no longer exists – which means if a child has a SEN that may lead them to lash out if their normal support is unavailable, they cannot be excluded for this. Reasonable adjustments must be in place.

Many acts of discrimination are not deliberate. They just involve individuals not thinking things through. This generally reminds me of the image below which, in its various formats, has been floating around the internet for a few years.

Where an individual believes that discrimination exists, they can appeal to the First Tier Tribunal for SEN cases, or the county court for all other cases.

It can be hard for schools (and parents) to understand that the equalities act requires people with certain characteristics to be treated more favourably than others, which seems to defy its title.

Let's take two children: Tom and Nell. Tom has a need that meets the definition of a disability. Nell does not. Both children are in the same class.

The teacher has just implemented a behaviour system where every child has three chances before receiving a break time detention for not completing work. Tom gets five chances.

The teacher uses the sad/smiley face system on the whiteboard. Students get one verbal warning before their name goes under the sad face. If they also get a tick next to their name they lose break time. Tom gets two verbal warnings and has to collect 3 ticks before he will serve the same sanction.

Both children have to travel from one side of the school to the other after PE. The school allows 3 minutes for this transition. Anyone who is late has to make the time up at the end of the day. Tom is allowed 10 minutes to make the transition.

Tom and Nell are both involved in bullying another student physically and verbally. They both say the same things, and both hit the other child the same way (with the same result). Tom is given a verbal warning; Nell serves a sanction.

With exclusions schools have to take care not to discriminate against any of the protected groups. We already know from the statistics that certain groups are over-represented in both permanent and fixed-term exclusions.

Examples of discriminatory exclusions include:

- Sending home a Sikh child for wearing their steel bracelets even where the school policy says no jewellery (religion) It should be noted that it may be reasonable to request they are removed or secured for certain activities

- Send home a girl for wearing trousers to school, although boys are allowed to wear them (sex)

- Refusing to allow a Y10 student to attend school because she is pregnant (pregnancy/maternity)

- Sending home an SEN child because their support is not available (SEN/Disability)

In the autumn of 2017, a 12-year-old student arrived on his first day of school at a school. However, his learning was cut short when he was pulled aside and informed that his hairstyle breached the school's uniform policy. He was told that he could either cut his dreadlocks off or face suspension. His mother, who had tied her son's hair so it did not violate the school's policy on hair length, cited the school's demand as religious discrimination and an attack on her family's Rastafarian culture. The family was supported in taking legal action against the school on the basis of religious discrimination. The legal case ended in an agreement between both parties that acknowledged the school's enforcement of its uniform policy resulted in indirect discrimination. The family was informed that he was welcome to return to the school "provided that his dreadlocks are tied up so that they do not touch the top of his collar or covered with a cloth of colour to be agreed by the school." However, the child had switched schools soon after the incident and has no intention of returning. According to his mother, he is now at a school that "accepts him for who he is."

Governors

There is often some confusion about who the governors are and who you are seeing.

Governance of schools is the largest voluntary body in the UK. None of the individuals who govern schools are paid for doing so. They have an eclectic mix of skills and experience. Because it is a voluntary role governing bodies tend to be made up from older individuals with time on their hands or those who work for companies which encourage voluntary action. Some governors will have fallen into the role as parents, whilst others used to work in education and still want to play a part. Whilst a governing body has a chair, they are all equal and no one individual vote holds more weight than another. The governors meet regularly to 'manage' the school. They are responsible for the vision and ethos and they hold the senior leaders (including the headteacher) to account, this means that whilst they have a relationship with the school they are not always on the 'side' of the school.

There are a few misconceptions about the roles of governors:

- The chair of governors might not be on a behaviour or exclusion panel
- A complaints governor cannot have been a part of the exclusions process
- The chair of governors might not be the person who deals with complaints
- Governors are volunteers often with full-time jobs and personal lives/holidays
- Those who attend any convened panel will be who is available
- Governors are not paid
- Governors are not on the side of the school
- They have the best interests of everyone involved in mind – their role is to ensure the vision and values of the school are achieved.
- Governors will have ratified the school behaviour policy and the school SEN policy
- At a panel we look at the process applied by the school and whether it was applied properly.

(…and yes, I've overturned a few decision in the past and told them to sort themselves out!)

Who

When you make an appeal or complaint to the governing body about an exclusion, they must have no prior knowledge of the incident or the child. This means that staff governors are unable to sit on exclusion panels.

Governors involved in the incident or who perhaps dealt with a parental complaint before it came to the panel should not be involved. (I do not deal with parental complaints; I have a complaints governor for this. If parents are unhappy with the solution it can then be escalated to me. It also means I can sit on an exclusions panel without having been influenced by previous information.)

The vast majority of schools will also have parent representation on their governing body. These individuals are not excluded from participating in exclusion panels, but if they have a direct interest in the result (for example your child is in the same class as their child or your child assaulted their child) then it would not be appropriate.

If you take your appeal to the IRP (independent review panel) then you have the option to appoint an SEN expert.

What is an SEN Expert?

You have the right to request an SEN expert attends an Independent Review Panel meeting regardless of whether the school recognises that your child has special educational needs.

The SEN expert appointed cannot have had any connection with the local authority, academy trust, you or your child or their siblings, or the incident leading to the exclusion. Working for the same local authority or trust does not automatically preclude an individual from serving as an SEN expert. (Which sounds contradictory but considering their sizes it is likely that they won't have come into contact.)

They provide impartial advice on how special educational needs might be relevant to the exclusion. The focus is on whether the school SEN policy is legal, reasonable and fair. They need to advise whether the school acted in a legal, reasonable and procedurally fair way in respect to the identification of special educational needs and any contribution that this could have made to the circumstances of the exclusion. They will not assess or diagnose your child and if your child displays differently to the majority of children with the same special educational need the SEN expert witness is not able to comment on this.

The SEN expert must have professional first-hand experience of the assessment and support of SEN and an understanding of the legal requirements on schools in relation to SEN and disability (I think I've found my next job).

It is recommended that the LA or MAT provide you with a choice of SEN experts, but neither side is able to meet them and discuss the case before the panel meeting. The LA or MAT meet the costs of this individual for the purposes of the meeting.

What they can do	What they cannot do
State how SEN might be relevant based on the evidence presented	Provide an assessment of your child
Look at the school policy and its application and state whether it is legal, reasonable and procedurally fair	Meet with you to discuss your child's specific needs
State whether the school should reasonably have identified any underlying SEN	Meet with the school to discuss how they work with SEN
State how the application of the policy might have affected the exclusion	Make suggestions about how they think things should be done

A letter to the governors

You are angry, frustrated and fed up! You also have a limited amount of time in which to turn things around and set the balls rolling should you wish to request a meeting with the governors/appeal against the decision. A well-constructed letter can be essential in getting your viewpoint across.

1. Give credit where credit is due. "Mr X tried to reason with...", "Fred apologised but..."

2. Stick to the point: <u>The Exclusion</u>. Whilst it would be nice to moan about the science teacher's dress sense, or the incident three years ago where a teacher ignored you, it is not relevant.

3. Be clear why it is unfair (awareness of needs). Have a look at the guidance below.

4. Give reasons how you believe the exclusion could be (have been) avoided.

5. Refer to statutory guidance including the Equality Act, any school policies and the exclusions guidance (available at the back of this book.)

- If the exclusion is related to your child's special educational needs use quotes from the CAFA (Children's and Families Act 2014). For example: Under S66 CAFA 2014 this has not been fulfilled, 'best endeavours to ensure SEN needs met by provision.' If your child has been permanently excluded copy, your letter to the Director of Children's Education at the local authority and state your 'expectations for a suitable full-time education to be arranged'.

What to consider when submitting your written evidence to appeal or complain:

PROCEDURE:	
Did the school follow the proper procedures in accordance with the guidance? Was it the head who decided to exclude the child? Were you notified in writing without undue delay?	Did the letter state the reason/s for the exclusion? Did your child have a say? Was alternative education provided?
LAWFUL:	
What are the reasons for the exclusion? Are they genuine disciplinary reasons?	Was the incident against the school's behaviour policy?
EVIDENCE:	
Was your child innocent? What is their version of the story? Do witnesses support their version? What does your child's school record indicate?	Are there any conflicts with statements from witnesses? Has your child been in trouble before? Is it likely they would behave this way? Are there any witness statements missing?
FAIR:	
Is the behaviour policy being applied consistently?	Are other children involved and how were they treated?
FACTORS:	
Was your child affected by other events at home or school?	Was this something the school was aware of?
SUPPORT:	
If this was a pattern of behaviour or there were other behaviour concerns has the school put in support to try and address this? Have they considered a multidisciplinary assessment?	Is there a plan in place? Has the support been reviewed?
SEN:	
How do your child's special educational needs affect their behaviour? Has the school followed its own SEN policy?	Was your child receiving the support they should have been? Was the incident a direct result of a lack of support?
DISCRIMINATION:	
Was the exclusion affected by something like race, gender, disability, sexual orientations? If you child has a disability is the behaviour they are being punished for a direct consequence of the disability?	Were there any reasonable adjustments a school could have made to avoid the incident? Give examples of how the school could have responded.
PROPORTIONATE:	
Is the punishment too severe for the offence? What alternatives are available?	Look at the school behaviour policy and the scale of punishments related to seriousness of offence.

By constructing your evidence using some, or all, of the headings above you will be able to present to the governors a clear argument against your child's exclusion.

Appeals

If you decide to appeal the decision of the headteacher to exclude then you will need to follow the correct process. Use the tables on the following pages to get an idea of what will happen.

Some special notes to be aware of:

Definitions	
Illegal	The headteacher or the governing body acted outside the scope of their legal power
Irrational	The governing body or headteacher relied on irrelevant points, failed to take account of all information or made an unreasonable decision
Procedural impropriety	The process was unfair or flawed. In the case of an IRP the only decision that can be made if this is found to be true, is to quash the decision and direct the governing body to consider again

Only the governing body and a first-tier tribunal can direct a school to reinstate a pupil. An IRP can only direct the governing body to reconsider its decision.

If told to reconsider its decision (by the IRP) then the governing body must reconvene within 10 days. If they are DIRECTED to reconsider but chose not to reinstate then they can be fined £4000 in addition to any money that will automatically follow the student for no longer being on role. A family can appeal to judicial review if the decision of the IRP is ignored.

Appealing Permanent Exclusion/15+/Exams

Notes

This process is used when the exclusion is **PERMANENT**
   Or, will take the total days of exclusion in a term **ABOVE 15**
   Or, if the exclusion will result in the student missing a public **EXAMINATION** or national curriculum test. *

Meeting held	Who is involved?
The meeting is automatically convened within 15 school days. You do not need to request the meeting. The meeting has to take place within this timescale and the availability of the governing body, so there may be some flexibility, but generally very little. You will be informed of the date of the meeting by either the school office or the clerk to the governors.	There will be a minimum of 3 governors – none of whom will have been involved in the exclusion. Staff governors are not permitted to be part of the panel. If any of the governors were involved in the reason for the exclusion or have involvement with the exclusion for another reason (e.g. a staff complaint) then they cannot be a part of the board. The headteacher is a governor but is not allowed to be a part of this panel. Governors will not have met and discussed the exclusion with the school before the meeting. Different exclusions might have different panel members and the chair of governors is not required to sit on the panel. A parent governor can sit on the panel, but they must not have a personal interest in the exclusion (e.g., your children are in the same class, or they were injured.)
Support	
The school must make arrangements to support you where appropriate, for example providing an interpreter. You can contact your local SENDIAS for support or if your child does not have special educational needs then you might consider asking a friend or relative to assist. There is a list of bodies which support with exclusions in the HELP section of this book.	The clerk will take minutes of the meeting and advise all attendees of the process and any legal considerations. The clerk is neutral, and you can ask for information. The Headteacher will attend to explain the school's reason for the exclusion. The parents are invited to make the case for your child, you do not have to attend, and you can submit in writing only if you prefer. The child is invited but does not need to attend. The local authority should be invited to permanent exclusion, although often they do not attend, for an academy you will have to request they are invited, and they are normally in observer capacity rather than being allowed to make contributions. Witnesses might be invited but it is more usual to read their statements

Purpose of meeting	Procedural information
To look at the facts on the balance of probabilities and consider whether the headteacher's decision was lawful, reasonable and procedurally fair. They have to consider the interests and circumstances of the excluded child and have regard to the interests of pupils and other people working in the school.	You need to submit your written evidence in advance of the meeting. You will receive an exclusions pack with all of the witness statements and other information that will be used in the meeting. Your evidence forms part of this pack. It should be sent to everyone 5 days before the meeting. The clerk will usually organise all of this. In some situations, new papers can be tabled at the meeting and a short break will be provided to read them. The governors on the panel will not have discussed the exclusion prior to the meeting with the headteacher or other school staff so they only have what is presented on paper or in the meeting
Possible outcomes	The meeting
Decline to reinstate Direct the school/headteacher to reinstate Make a note on the child's file Allow the child to sit examinations	The chair will welcome everyone and make introductions The chair will explain what will happen and the possible outcomes The headteacher will present the school's case for the exclusion The parent will present their case against the exclusion All parties will be allowed to ask questions The headteacher will be asked for a summary The parents will be asked for a summary The parents and headteacher will leave the room and the governors will discuss the evidence presented. The clerk will stay to advise on any notes made or legal matters.
Making their decision	
The governors can only use the evidence presented in the meeting. If they believe the school has acted unlawfully, unreasonably, or has not followed its own procedures correctly then they can direct the school to reinstate the student.	
Being informed	
Most governing boards will give you their response following a discussion and follow this up in writing. Where they expect the discussion to take a long time, they may suggest you leave, and they will contact you later. They must give you their response in writing and it should clearly state the outcome and their reasons. If you feel that your child has a disability that they have not taken into account, then you can make a disability discrimination claim to the **First Tier Tribunal SEND.**	

PERMANENT EXCLUSION		
If the governing body disagree with the school	**If the governing body agree with the school**	**If you disagree with the outcome**
They will direct the school to reinstate the child to the school. You may decide that you do not want your child to return to this school, in which case a note will be put on their file so that the next school is aware the exclusion was overturned.	The process to remove your child from the school roll will begin. As the meeting is likely to be after the 6th day of the exclusion, then your child will need to continue to attend the local authority arranged provision. The school cannot remove your child from the role until 15 days have passed (time for you to appeal to the IRP) or if you indicate you will not be appealing. An appeal to the first-tier tribunal for discrimination will not delay the removal from the school role.	You have 15 days to lodge an appeal to an **independent review panel.** If disability discrimination is involved, you can appeal to the **first-tier tribunal SEND.** Where the equalities act has been breached (e.g. race or religion) then an appeal can be lodged to the **county court**. These have different time scales (usually 6 months from the date of the alleged discrimination.
FIXED TERM 15+ DAYS		
If the governing body disagree with the school	**If the governing body agree with the school**	**If you disagree with the outcome**
They will direct the school to reinstate the child to the school.	The exclusion remains on your child's record and they return to the school after the exclusion. If any alternative provision has been organised, then your child must attend this.	As above

*EXAMINATIONS – this is the only exclusion where a single member of the governing body can make an emergency decision. It is usually the chair of governors and they can make the decision without holding a meeting if convening a meeting will result in a delay that might affect the examinations taking place.

If the governing body disagree with the school	If the governing body agree with the school	If you disagree with the outcome
They will direct the school to reinstate the child to the school and take their examinations.	The exclusion remains on your child's record and they return to school after the exclusion. If any alternative provision has been organised, then your child must attend this.	As above

The governing body or the school may decide to allow your child to sit any examinations during an exclusion. This might be conducted away from the normal venue. They are under no obligation to organise this.

What you need to do before the meeting

You need to prepare your written evidence as to why your child should not be excluded. You need to convince the governors that the decision to exclude your child was not lawful, reasonable or fair. See [A letter to the governors]
Make sure you have collected all the paperwork in the PARENT PROCEDURE section of this book.

Appealing
Fixed-Term Exclusion 6-14 days

Notes

This process is used when the exclusion is **FIXED-TERM** and between **6-14 DAYS** in a term. Several shorter exclusions can be used to make up this number.

Meeting held	Invited
The meeting is convened within 50 school days of your request. Governors will not normally convene a meeting without you requesting one although they are aware of the exclusions (not the names) from their meetings.	There will be a minimum of 3 governors – none of whom will have been involved in the exclusion. Staff governors are not permitted to be part of the panel. If any of the governors were involved in the reason for the exclusion or have involvement with the exclusion for another reason (e.g. a staff complaint) then they cannot be a part of the board. The headteacher is a governor but is not allowed to be a part of this panel. The clerk will take minutes of the meeting and advise all attendees of the process and any legal considerations. The clerk is neutral, and you can ask for information.
Support	The headteacher will attend to explain the school's reason for the exclusion
The school must make arrangements to support you where appropriate, for example providing an interpreter.	The parents are invited to make the case for your child, you do not have to attend, and you can submit in writing only if you prefer. The child is invited but does not need to attend.

Purpose of meeting	Procedural information	The meeting
To look at the facts on the balance of probabilities and consider whether the headteacher's decision was lawful, reasonable and procedurally fair.	You need to submit your written evidence in advance of the meeting. You will receive an exclusions pack with all statements and other information that will be used. Your evidence forms part of this pack In some situations, new papers can be tabled at the meeting and a short break will be provided to read them.	The process is the same as for a permanent exclusion meeting.
Possible outcomes		
Agree with the school Disagree with the school Make a note on the child's file.		

Making their decision	Being informed	
The governors can only use the evidence presented in the meeting. If they believe the school has acted unlawfully, unreasonably, or has not followed its own procedures correctly then they can direct the school to reinstate the student.	Most governing boards will give you their response following a discussion and follow this up in writing. Where they expect the discussion to take a long time, they may suggest you leave, and they will contact you later. They must give you their response in writing and it should clearly state the outcome and their reasons. If you feel that your child has a disability that they have not taken into account, then you can make a disability discrimination claim to the **First Tier Tribunal SEND**.	
If the governing body disagree with the school	**If the governing body agree with the school**	**If you disagree with the outcome**
They will direct the school to make a note on the child's file that the exclusion was overruled in a governing body meeting. They are not likely to be able to change the exclusion as the time scale will have passed and the codes cannot be changed. A note will explain to any new school that the 'E' was overruled. You may have already removed your child to another school in which case a note will be appended that the exclusion was overturned.	No further action is required by the governing body.	You have 15 days to lodge an appeal to an **independent review panel**. If disability discrimination is involved, you can appeal to the **first-tier tribunal SEND**. Where the equalities act has been breached (e.g. race or religion) then an appeal can be lodged to the **county court**. These have different time scales (usually 6 months from the date of the alleged discrimination.
What you need to do before the meeting		
As with a permanent exclusion you will need to submit in writing why you disagree with the exclusion. See [A letter to the governors]		

Appealing Fixed-term Exclusion up to 5 days

Notes		
This process is used when the exclusion is **FIXED-TERM** and **LESS THAN 5 DAYS**		
Meeting held within	**Invited**	**Not invited**
You have the right to put your views in writing to the governors and they must consider these but there is no set time limit and they do not have to arrange to meet with you.	No one – the governing body is not required to meet with you	N/A
^	^	**Support**
^	^	As the school is not convening a meeting, they are not required to provide you with support.
Purpose of meeting	**Possible outcomes**	**The meeting**
To look at the facts on the balance of probabilities and consider whether the headteacher's decision was lawful, reasonable and procedurally fair.	The governors do not have the power to reinstate your child and it is likely they will be back in school anyway. The 'E' on the register cannot be removed, but if the governors agree with you it was not justified, they may put a note on the school record.	The governors may meet to discuss your written representation, but they do not need to meet with you. They may decide to hold an informal meeting to explain their decision.
If the governing body disagree with the school	**If the governing body agree with the school**	**If you disagree with the outcome**
They will direct the school to add a note to your child's file to explain the exclusion.	Nothing will change.	You will need to use the school complaints system
What you need to do		
You need to prepare your written evidence as to why your child should not be excluded. You need to convince the governors that the decision to exclude your child was not lawful, reasonable or fair.		

Appealing
Independent Review Panel (IRP)

Notes	
If you disagree with the decision of the governing body of the school, then you can appeal to an independent review panel (IRP). You cannot appeal because you did not like their decision, it has to be based on them having acted **illegally**, **irrationally** or **improperly**.	
Meeting held within	**Invited & Panel Members**
You must state that you want to go to an independent review within 15 school days of the original governing body decision. The panel will meet within 15 days of the request.	The panel members are not members of the school. They have no links with the school or the family. There will be either 3 or 5 panel members. There must be: 1x Lay person (someone who has no school experience) + 1 or 2 school governors with 12 months experience in the last 5 years and have not been a teacher or headteacher in this time. + 1 or 2 headteachers or have been headteachers in the last 5 years. Where possible the headteachers will represent the phase of education of your child (primary or secondary). All panel members will have attended training within the last 2 years. In addition, there will be a clerk who will take minutes and coordinate communications. They also attend training and usually have a sound legal knowledge around exclusions. If you request one, an SEN expert witness can be invited. This person must not know your child, or the school and their attendance is paid for by the LA or MAT. They can only advise on special educational needs in general and not how they specifically affect your child. The parent The school
Who organises?	
Local authority-maintained schools have their IRP arranged by the local authority. Academies have their IRP arranged by the trust. The clerk will communicate matters with you. Any costs are met by the LA or MAT.	
Purpose of meeting	**Procedural information**
To review the decision of the governing body by looking at the illegality, irrationality and impropriety (of procedure) of their decision	You need to submit your written evidence in advance of the meeting. You should be able to submit anything you had previously alongside the reasons for your appeal. Remember you can't appeal just because you disagree with the decision – you will need to demonstrate that the governing body acted in a way that was illegal, irrational or procedurally improper.

Possible outcomes	It is important to realise that this panel cannot overturn the decision. They can direct the GB to reconsider...but they don't have to!	
Uphold the decision of the governing body (this will be the case for anything that is not illegal, irrational or improper) Recommend the governing body reconsider Quash and direct the governing body to reconsider	The meeting itself will be similar in structure to the governing body meeting with the panel listening to each side in turn and asking questions Both sides can table new information, but the panel can only consider what was available (or should have been available) to the governors at the time of their decision. The school can table new evidence, but it cannot change its reasons for the exclusion.	
If the panel disagree with the school + GB	**If the panel agree with the school**	**If you disagree with the outcome**
They will direct the governing body to reconsider their decision within 10 school days. The governing body may decide to stick with their guns. Where there has been procedural impropriety the panel can quash the decision and direct the school to reconsider. Again, the school has 10 school days. If they choose not to reinstate then the IRP can fine the school, but the exclusion will still stand. You would need to take this to a **Judicial Review**	No further action is required by the governing body.	There is no further right to appeal. You can complain. This may result in a further IRP (to review the decision of the original IRP) but the exclusion decision cannot be overturned. If you believe the panel was maladministered then: Complaints about maintained schools should be made to the local authority Ombudsman 0300 061 0614 Complaints about academies should be made to the Secretary of State and the ESFA – 0370 0002288. Complaints must be made within 1 year of the decision. If you think their decision was flawed, then you need to apply to the High Court for a judicial review within 3 months.

Appealing
Judicial Review

Notes

If the IRP has directed a governing body to reconsider the exclusion but the governing body has decided to uphold their original decision, then there is no right to a second IRP. You can take this to a judicial review.

If you feel that the IRP has been maladministered then you will take this to judicial review or the LGO. The Governing body might also conclude that the IRP was maladministered and can bring action against them.

Meeting held within	Bring the JR against the GB if...	Bring the JR against the IRP if...
A judicial review must be held within 3 months of you lodging the appeal. **Who attends?** For a judicial review you will need legal representation. The JR will decide who needs to attend the hearing.	Following a direction from the IRP to reinstate the governing body uphold the exclusion by: • Making an error in law • Being unreasonable • Breaching natural justice	• The constitution of the panel was incorrect • The panel relied on school information now shown to be false • The parent was not allowed to participate • The parent was not given proper notice

Purpose of review	Possible Outcomes
The court will look at the lawfulness of the decision.	They can overturn the decision or direct a new appeal hearing

A judicial review would be very specific to your set of circumstances and a generic response here would be inappropriate and inaccurate

Appealing
First Tier Tribunal SEND

Notes

If you believe your child has been discriminated against because of their special educational need or disability you can bring an appeal to the first-tier tribunal SEND. This is the same body that meet to hear complaints about the EHC process.

Your child must meet the definition of 'disabled' for this route to be taken and can be used for fixed-term and permanent exclusions.

Meeting held within	Reasons to bring an appeal to the first-tier tribunal
Claims must be lodged within 6 months of the date of exclusion. With a permanent exclusion the tribunal will aim to fast track any appeals usually within 6 weeks.	• The school has failed to make accommodation for identified special educational needs which led to an excludable incident (reasonable adjustments) • The school treated the child unfavourably because of their special educational needs
Who attends?	**Notes**
For a first-tier tribunal you do not need legal representation, but it is recommended. The tribunal will decide who needs to attend the hearing.	• A school does not have to demonstrate that it has applied EVERY possible reasonable adjustment, but it does need to show that it has taken reasonable steps with due regard to financial impact, practicality and reducing substantial disadvantage.
Purpose of review	**Possible Outcomes**
The court will look at the whether any disability discrimination has taken place.	The tribunal has the power to order that the child is reinstated into school. It can also request a 'declaration' (admission of error), 'apology' or 'policy change'

A first-tier tribunal would be very specific to your set of circumstances and a generic response here would be inappropriate and inaccurate

Parental responsibility

"How does it feel to be expelled from home school?"

It is of no doubt that your child's exclusion is inconvenient. If you are a working parent, school usually acts as your day care and when your child is no longer allowed to attend this can cause difficulties.

If you are asked to collect your child from school early then, the chances are your work is already aware of a developing situation; whether you have declared that as a medical emergency or told them the truth is entirely up to you.

With shorter exclusions most parents are able to take emergency parental leave from work, reshuffle shifts to take a last-minute holiday day, and you may even be lucky enough to have relatives or friends who can step in.

With longer exclusions, frequent short exclusions or a permanent exclusion, the goodwill of your work colleagues and relations can quickly become strained. Over 50% of parents of children who display challenging behaviours find themselves having to give up work or take sustained periods of unpaid leave. This in itself can add strains to the family.

The letter from the school has a serious tone which clearly states your parental responsibilities during the exclusion. It is certainly worth reading the letter or this chapter so you fully understand what you can and cannot do. The last thing you will want is a financial penalty on top of the exclusion.

Not in school during an exclusion

If your child is excluded from the school, then they will not expect to see them on site. This includes when you are collecting siblings from school. The school may opt to be helpful and deliver your other children to the gate or perhaps keep them slightly later so that you can collect them with your 'excluded' child after the end of the school day. However, they do not have to do this. As inconvenient as it is, you may have to make separate arrangements to collect your other children from school.

Sometimes this is to protect your child as much as anything else; emotions can run raw.

My child was permanently excluded for breaking the arm of another child in his class. When I arrived at school to collect his younger brother the parent of the other child came over and started screaming at my son demanding to know why he was there.

School disco? Sorry, if your child is excluded then that also means from any special events even though they are 'out of school time'. It is worth asking the school on this though, since if your other children are involved in a school concert which you wish to attend as a guest, then depending on the reason why your other child was excluded the school may allow you both to attend.

My Y3 daughter had a role in the school nativity. She was excluded. She was not allowed to attend and take part. My Y5 daughter also had a role in her Christmas play, I was allowed to take my Y3 daughter to watch the play.

School trip? Again, if the exclusion coincides with a school trip then your child will not be going. If you have paid for the trip, then it is up to the school whether or not the place is refunded. As most trips are heavily subsidised by schools and places will have been booked in advance it is unlikely that a refund will be issued.

My son was excluded for 2 days. The second coincided with the date they were supposed to go on their 3-day residential. School said he couldn't go, and he wasn't allowed to join them in the evening. They said I could take him over for the second day of the residential. The school were actually correct in not allowing him to join them in the evening of the excluded day, his attendance on the school register would have been marked as E and not as V.

Absence

Sorry, an exclusion is an absence however you wish to look at it even though it has been enforced upon you. It is however classed as an <u>authorised absence</u> and is coded as E on the registers. Sometimes, it might be coded as B if home education/tutor provided or as a D if dual registered with an AP. Normal registration marks are: / am \ pm and V if they are on a school visit (might be used if you go to visit another school)

There is a specific circumstance where a school can exclude your child without recording it as an E...and this is where they have a communicable illness. The NHS produces guidelines about the amount of time children should have off from school for common childhood illnesses. This serves to protect the other children and staff in the school.

Please don't send a child in who has sickness/diarrhoea and then complain when the teacher is off with the same! NHS guidance says 48 hours from the last episode and no swimming for 2 weeks following. Schools sometimes relax this to 24 hours, although having seen some rather nasty tummy bugs rip through schools (I once taught a class where only 3 out of 30 made it in and one of those we sent home) I'd rather the NHS guides were followed.

https://www.nhs.uk/live-well/healthy-body/is-my-child-too-ill-for-school/

https://www.gov.uk/government/publications/health-protection-in-schools-and-other-childcare-facilities/chapter-9-managing-specific-infectious-diseases

I often see parents complain about an attendance letter sent home and I'd like to take the opportunity to clarify a few points on these.

1. They are usually centrally generated, by a computer system and enveloped up by office staff who will not be privy to your child's personal reasons for absence. They simply collate the prints and post them out.

2. Absence is absence. If your child is not in school, it is an absence. Regardless of the reason. Some absences are authorised, some are unauthorised.

3. Exclusions are an absence and count towards the absence total. They are authorised absences. If these are the only absences on the record, then the school cannot threaten you with fines. However, if your child has also had absences for illness, holidays or medical visits then their persistent absenteeism figure will be high and additional absences may be under scrutiny.

4. Students are classed as persistent absentees if they miss 10% or more of taught

sessions, this is 19 or more full days of school. Around 10-14% of students are classed as persistent absentees.

5. The national average for attendance is around the 95% mark, it varies by age of child and year on year, depending on how strong that year's flu bug was!

6. Schools are required to report their absence and persistent absentee figures – and to show how they are working to bring them down, hence you get the letter to inform you of the absence.

Attendance letters are usually accompanied by a print of your child's record. This can be very useful in determining whether exclusions are being recorded correctly.

Exams

When a child is excluded near to their examination this can bring an added stress. Where a child should be sitting external examinations, the school is under NO obligation to make arrangements for them to sit those exams. They do have to inform their governing body immediately and the governing body have to meet within 15 days and consider the exclusion and whether they will make arrangements for the child to sit the exams. Where it isn't feasible to convene a timely meeting because the exam is imminent then the chair of governors can review the decision alone (and report back at the next full governing body meeting about any decision made.)

The vast majority of schools will make arrangements for your child to sit exams – usually on a separate site, or in a separate location on site.

Tom and Nell were at loggerheads. Whereas, Nell was able to get on in school, Tom was stirring up trouble and winding up the other students. The school wanted to exclude him, but he was due to sit his GCSEs. They decided to use a combination of 5-day exclusion, study leave and provision off-site to complete his examinations. The school made appropriate arrangements with the exam board for the papers to be used at a different location and an invigilator was employed solely for Tom's exams.

This is generally applied to terminal public examinations (GCSEs) but is equally applicable to the statutory assessments in Y1 (phonics), Y2 (KS1 SATs), Y6 (KS2 SATs) and soon Y4 (Times table checks). Since some parents (and indeed some schools) opt out of these assessments it is less likely that alternative arrangements will be made. Truthfully, missing these has little lasting impact on your child.

Public spaces

In the exclusion letter there is a line about excluded children not being seen in a public space.

> Since your child is of compulsory school age, you have a duty to ensure that your child is not present in a public place during school hours for the duration of this exclusion [specify dates] unless there is reasonable justification for this. I must inform you that you may be prosecuted or receive a fixed penalty notice from the local authority if your child is present in a public place during school hours on the specified dates. It will be for you to show that there is reasonable justification.

It does not mean that you all need to hide in the house with the curtains drawn for the exclusion! It quite simply means that you can't let Tom or Nell go to the park to play or nip to the corner shop for you during school hours. They just can't do things that they would not normally be able to do during school time.

If you need to go to the corner shop, then you can take them with you. If you have a doctors' appointment, drag them along. If you have a job interview, take them over to Nan's.

Technically, my student who took the trip to Alton Towers would have been subject to a penalty notice if the truancy officers had caught him as this was not a reasonable justification.

I took son number 3 to a soft play centre soon after son number 4 was born for a birthday treat at 11 am on a Friday morning. I live in a different authority to the soft play centre and our INSET days did not line up. The soft play centre questioned our attendance, asked my son his school and phoned them to confirm it was indeed an INSET day. If he had been excluded this would not have been a reasonable justification for our presence. However, if I had been attending with the younger one for a pre-arranged play-date and I wasn't allowing my elder son to 'play' then this could have been a justified presence in a public space.

Quite simply, this is a grey area, apply some common sense. And whilst it is the school that gave you the letter it is not them dictating the law!

The different perspectives

The national view & effectiveness of exclusion

Exclusion; it is a life-changing event

For some students the brief shock of an exclusion may well be enough to ensure they are on the right road and never receive another exclusion again. I believe that this is true…for some children.

However, the statistics tell us a slightly different story.

- 74% children in PRUs are persistent absentees. (The national average is between 10-14%)
- Only 1% achieved 5 good GCSEs
- Over 40% are NEET (Not in Education, Employment or Training) at age 16
- 85% of individuals in youth offending institutes have been excluded
- A PRU placement costs in the region £33000/year
- 50% of the adult prison population have experienced school exclusion (Making the Difference 2017 from the Institute for Public Policy Research)
- 29% of the prison population had an identified learning difficulty or SEND (Prison Reform Trust 2017)

So, for those children who needed a short, sharp shock an exclusion may well work. For many others it sets them in a cycle of failure and can have lifelong implications. I am not for one moment suggesting that your child, who has just been excluded, will be one of the numbers above – there are many, many factors at play in shaping a young person, but it is important to know the facts and information.

For students who are permanently excluded twice in 2 years the story is more complicated since no admission authority (local authority or academy trust) is compelled to admit them to roll even where spaces exist.

The Student perspective

Some students see an exclusion as a badge of honour,
for others it is a medal of shame,
Some will see it as the ultimate punishment,
whilst others feel it is the definitive reward.
...but they probably won't admit to that!

Children who experience fixed-term exclusions have to go back to their school. For some this is no different than returning after a couple of days off with a cold or sickness bug. Depending on the reason for their exclusion there may even be some kudos with their classmates. Whereas, with younger children or those in very large secondary schools their classmates might not even have noticed!

Other children will find the return very difficult and the reintegration is important. The exclusion is a raw wound that can be easily damaged with a careless comment. Some will be embarrassed by their behaviour or actions; others will be resentful of the staff or witnesses involved.

Students who enjoy school are less likely to reoffend as they do not want to miss it.

Students who are having a difficult time at school may feel that the exclusion is a necessary relief and welcome the opportunity to have an authorised absence.

Children who are permanently excluded do not have that opportunity to return and rebuild bridges, instead they are thrown into a new world, a new school, a new set of expectations.

Many students do not understand the repercussions of a permanent exclusion and speaking with many children in PRUs they are under the impression that they will be returning to their school at some point.

The vast majority of children can identify why they were excluded:

"I've always had bad temper, always. At the time when I am angry, I think this is horrible. When I calmed down ... what idiot I've been and why did I do it, just WHY did I go to that level, extreme, when I could have done it in another way. But, it's just like instinct, for me, for some reason."

"Because of my behaviour... they just couldn't keep controlling of me basically."

"Hmm, I think that I did just a little thing and that was my last chance. It was not just a major thing, it was lots and lots of little things really and then they just couldn't, and they've decided to kick me out basically in the end, because they gave me too many chances."

"Obviously in my eyes I don't think it's fair because it's me. Obviously, I don't want to kick myself out. But, I don't know ... maybe they think that they gave me enough chances and it was time to kick me out probably they did, they gave me enough chances. Yeah, probably it was fair."

Schools offer a unique social opportunity and the comment made most frequently by students who have been excluded is not to do with their education, but that they miss their friends and the opportunity for social interactions.

The Parent perspective

"Let me see if Billy is in our database... Oh my! He's a Code Red!"

Families are deeply affected by exclusion. Some feel ashamed of their child's behaviour whilst others feel let down by the system.

In primary schools where the child is the one the teacher asks to 'have a word about' at the end of the day, the parents can be embarrassed, often leading to isolation. They frequently report that they think they are blamed or stigmatised for their child's behaviour and that they are only contacted for negative incidents. Where a child has been a concern for a while, the parent may have been offering advice to the school and feel that this has not been acted on. This all impedes the communication between schools and families.

And, like all parents, we come equipped with our own pair of rose-tinted blinkers.

Belonging to a couple of parent groups on Facebook I ended up in both sides of an argument once.

GROUP 1

Tom went into school and his teacher was absent. Mum warned the school that he was rather excited about a birthday party he was going to later that day. Tom spent all day displaying hyper behaviour. At lunchtime, he squirted some of his juice over the table and floor, whilst his TA was getting a cloth to wipe it up Tom decided to pour the rest of his juice over Nell's head. Nell screamed at Tom. Tom responded by telling her to 'shut the **** up'. When the TA came back with the cloth, Nell told her what had happened and Tom threw himself over the table to attack Nell, pulling her hair and kicking her in the shins. Nell pushed Tom away and he slipped on the juice spill banging his head on the floor.

Tom's Mum: I don't think it's his fault. I told them he was excited. He won't be able to go to the party now.

School: Tom's behaviour has deteriorated throughout the day despite us assigning a TA to him 1:1 all day. We are going to exclude him for 1 day for verbal abuse and violence towards another student.

Tom's Mum: I hate that school they never listen to me! I'm going to take him to the zoo tomorrow, I'm not punishing him as well and he missed the party because of the bump on his head. The other kid shoved my Tommy and I bet she doesn't get excluded.

GROUP 2

Nell went into school and her teacher was absent. Mum explained that her dog had died last night and that she had been up all-night crying. Nell spent the morning feeling very sad. She had a headache. At lunchtime, she didn't really want to go in the lunch hall. Tom was being noisy and called her a cry baby. She told him to go away and be quiet. She'd been telling him to do that all morning. He poured his drink over her head. Nell didn't like this. She screamed and cried louder. Tom was rude to her. Nell waited for the TA to come back and told her. Tom didn't like it, so he hit her. Nell felt scared and pushed him away. He fell over and banged his head.

Nell's Mum: I don't think it's her fault. I told them she was upset.

School: Nell has been given lots of support today and we recognise that she felt threatened by the other child, but she did cause an injury when she retaliated. Yes, we can see the bruises on her shins and the other child is receiving an exclusion too. We are going to exclude her for ½ day for violence towards another student.

Nell's Mum: It's bloody ridiculous, she was only defending herself! It's that damned Tom he's always causing trouble and gets away with it.

Both parents are guilty of wearing the rose-tinted glasses and feeling that their child was in the right, but on examining both sides of the story neither child was treated unfairly. In fact, the school had gone out of its way to make sure that they were both fully supported. Sometimes, we need to take a step back and realise that our children are not little angels all the time and that behaviours do have consequences.

Whether I agree they should have been excluded is a different matter. Without knowing the history of both children, it does seem a little extreme. They could have spent some time in reparation with each other...but maybe the school knows a little more of the story than the two Facebook groups were privy to. No doubt, Nell would be happier getting rid of her headache at home.

When children are permanently excluded, or where they begin to rack up lots of fixed-term exclusions. parents are naturally anxious as to the future and the possible outcomes for their child.

In 2017, 83.8% of children in a group of surveyed schools achieved 5 A*-C GCSES (the grading system has since changed). Only 47.5% of children with exclusions related to their behaviour achieved the same. This can have massive life-long implications in terms of access to college courses, training and employment.

When a child is regularly excluded or where they have been permanently excluded but a placement has not been established then some parents find themselves forced into giving up work, making themselves 'unemployed' to sufficiently care for their child. This causes difficulties with claiming benefits since the decision to leave their position of work was theirs and not some outside factor. These families end up having to consider some serious financial implications. Around 50% of families who experience several fixed-term exclusions or a permanent exclusion find at least one member of the family has to give up work, and 37% 'get into trouble at work' for the amount of time they have to take off.

This was recently posted this on Twitter: "Families are driven into poverty and pupils isolated when excluded pupils have no school place." This was in response to the newspaper articles reporting the clamping down on unregistered schools. (Barbara Ball, April 2019)

We know that most families do not fight exclusions, perhaps because they are unclear of their rights. Those that do face battles in challenging exclusions, securing appropriate provision, and sourcing information, all of which is mentally exhausting.

The School perspective

Scarily, the Children's Commissioner, Anne Longfield, recently issued a post in which she stated that 88% of all exclusions are issued by just 10% of all schools (with a similar pattern across all local authorities.)

One school, in July 2018, had OFSTED pay a visit. Their exclusions accounted for 50% of the local authority total. They had 2257 incidences recorded resulting in 2431 days of lost learning through fixed-term exclusions in the academic year to that point (with 541 in May and June alone). It was the equivalent of every child in their school receiving 3 exclusions, the majority of which were children with SEN. In addition, they also had 7 permanent exclusions and 8 families had opted for elective home education. The school blamed its accumulative consequences system. Can I reiterate the point that this whole paragraph is referencing just ONE school?

So, some schools struggle with exclusions more than others.

If exclusions must happen, transition plans and open communication links should be provided

Schools need to employ a culture of inclusion rather than a zero-tolerance

Exclusions need to be put back to their rightful place as the ultimate sanction, instead of a method to secure support for a child

I'm not one for giving teachers excuses. There was no behaviour management or information about SEN when I trained to be a teacher, and no one sent me on a magical course to inform my practise once I started teaching. 80% is common sense and the other 20% is made up from experience and wider reading. That said, not every teacher can be expected to know how to handle every child that crosses their path. I'll admit to throwing the rule book out on occasions and working in the dark, adapting things as I go. But then, I've never been driven by trying to achieve an outstanding OFSTED grading or a perfect set of exam results (now you know why I was never a headteacher). Instead, I believe that once a child's name is on my register it is my responsibility to make my classroom somewhere they want to be, somewhere they can thrive and not a battleground. And I admit, I sometimes make mistakes!

Deviating from my two names, meet Daniel.

Daniel was a pain in the backside, (no other words for it) and I was an NQT (newly qualified teacher). Every day, I felt he was trying to ruin my lessons. Every day, I went back in and tried again with him. I'll never forget my mentor's (bad) advice on one occasion.

Me: Daniel, you know it's really tiring having to restart the lesson over and over because of your behaviour. Do you think that tomorrow we could aim for ten minutes before you shout out or throw something?

My mentor (in front of Daniel): I don't know why your bothering, he won't change. You should just give up on him, kick him out into the corridor and get on with your lesson. That's what I do.

Me: I don't think that's fair; Daniel has a right to be in his class, and it's cold in the corridor.

Daniel (interrupting): Yeah, that's why I was running up and down this morning.

Mentor: Yes, and that's why if you keep being a pain, I'm going to have you excluded. I only have to send you out 3 more times and it'll be a 5-day exclusion. (We had a tariff of sent outs adding up to exclusions.)

The following day.

Daniel(lining up outside the room):Miss, can I ask something?

Me: Yeah, sure, what's up?

Daniel: Will we have to copy off the board when we go in today?

Me: Yes, you know that's how we start every lesson, why? (School policy was to have the objectives on the board for the class to copy along with a paragraph of text about the lesson for handwriting practise...every lesson!)

Daniel (whispering): Can you help me? I can't see it properly and the words get muddled.

On entering the classroom, we had a quick shuffle of seats and Daniel ended up near the front, where I just happened to leave my teacher notes. I didn't get ten minutes of work from Daniel, I got a whole lesson, and the next, and the next. What a shame my mentor wouldn't listen to this breakthrough – she had him in the corridor and I couldn't help Daniel avoid his exclusion...but he set me on the path as a SENCO to help all the other Daniel's. Thank you, Daniel!

Schools have to set rules and boundaries just as are set in society. It wouldn't be acceptable to walk into the local supermarket and thump someone because you didn't like the way they looked at you. Nor would it be appropriate to carry a knife to the local sports centre because you feel threatened. Regardless of an individual's needs they do need to know right from wrong and schools have a role to play in educating them. Alongside this the rest of society expects to feel safe and individuals in a school should do so too.

That fence I sit on is incredibly wobbly at times, and one of those is over the recent case law where the exclusion of an ASC child was determined to be unlawful because reasonable adjustments hadn't been available. The child had assaulted their TA several times and, on the day, their regular TA had not been available their violent outburst had been extreme. The court ruled that additional support would have been a reasonable adjustment and may have prevented the outburst.

This was a tricky situation for all involved. The TA had a right to go to school without fear of being assaulted on a daily basis. The school had failed to provide an alternative when this member of staff was absent (I don't know the school, but perhaps the other staff were reluctant to be on the receiving end of the violent outbursts, I'm sure none of us really blame them.) The child hadn't learned that assaulting members of staff was unacceptable. So, was it really unfair of the school to exclude this child? And even more so, was it right of the court to overturn that exclusion meaning that a case law now exists that allows children who 'may display extreme behaviour as a result of their disability cannot be excluded for that even where it includes acts of extreme violence against the staff and students around them?'

My fence wobbles.

Whilst I can very clearly see that the child is exhibiting extreme behaviour that isn't entirely in their control, the message that is being given is that 'this behaviour is OK'.

I personally feel that a change of school to one which had the expertise and staffing to handle this child was needed and that the school in question probably had its hands tied in terms of accessing that without excluding the child.

Exclusions are on the increase for acts of violence. A recent (2019) survey of teachers found that violence by pupils affects 24 per cent of teachers at least once a week, and 4 per cent daily. 89 per cent had suffered physical or verbal abuse from pupils in the past year, while 86 per cent had been sworn at and 42 per cent verbally threatened.

It also found that over the same period:

- 29 per cent had been hit, punched or kicked;
- 39 per cent had been shoved or barged;
- 7 per cent had been spat at;
- 3 per cent had been head-butted.

In addition, 27 percent of teachers said they had had their property damaged.

Whilst I'm not the biggest fan of exclusions, no member of staff goes to work to face any of this.

The future (for your child)

Exclusion does little to improve behaviour, aggravates alienation from school and places some young people at risk of getting involved in anti-social behaviour or crime.
Not Present and Not Correct. Barnardo's

Exclusion is often seen as a last resort and there is sometimes the hope that a short-sharp shock will enable a child to see the error of their ways and 'change'. Whilst this may be true for some children who have been influenced to follow the wrong path, there is increasing evidence that there is a wider impact of exclusions for most, including those with special educational needs. Research suggests that the exclusions can be extremely harmful in the long run, with a large percentage of those excluded suffering from mental health issues that will be exacerbated by the measure, and many more ending up unemployed or in prison. (I'm not saying that is going to happen to your child, but that's just what the research by the University of Exeter suggests.)

When a student is excluded, they experience a sense of powerlessness over their situation and for some they try to seek that power in other areas. There is the chicken and egg question; are mental health difficulties and challenging behaviours the cause of the exclusion or is the exclusion the cause of the mental health difficulties and challenging behaviours?

Whilst the Barnardo's report is nearly 10 years old now, it makes some pertinent points around the exclusion.

- The estimate lifetime cost of a permanent exclusion is £65000
- A place for a pupil in a PRU is upwards of £15000 /year (current estimates state £33000)

- Removal from school may be the only option for severe discipline problems; when the safety of students and teachers is at risk, exclusion has to remain an option
- The students who undergo extended or repeated exclusions are the ones that need more supervision and not less
- Long term harm can result from being rejected by school
- Schools sometimes saw fixed-term exclusion as 'nipping problems in the bud'.
- Children sometimes appreciated what they saw as a few days off school but become quickly bored at home and families are often described as devastated.
- Pupils fall behind and find the return to school socially awkward after a few days of exclusion. Old relationship problems are still there on their return.
- While excluded the inclination of the young person to do the work unsupervised was negligible, given that they were already disaffected with school and usually among the least motivated students.
- For a few, exclusion may have been the short sharp shock that they needed to reflect on and improve their behaviour in the future.
- Permanently excluded students are three times more likely than their peers to leave school with no qualifications and over a third are more likely to be unemployed.
- It is a cause for concern that persistent disruptive behaviour is cited as the reason for permanent exclusion…this indicates that poor behaviour has been allowed to drift on when timely intervention could have avoided further disruption and helped address the underlying causes, rather than letting the difficulties becomes entrenched.
- There is a complacency around the use of fixed-term exclusions.

For children who really struggle at school, exclusion can be a relief as it removes them from an unbearable situation with the result that on their return to school they will behave even more badly to escape again. As such, it becomes an entirely counterproductive disciplinary tool as for these children it encourages the very behaviour that it intends to punish. Professor Ford. University of Exeter.

Me and Controversy

As if I'd ever be controversial! These are my opinions.

1. Some parents do need to accept that their child is not an innocent little angel and that they have actually done something wrong. I'd love to believe my children are angels...they're not!

2. Schools prepare children for society and life in general. Some behaviours would put the child in prison (or at risk of retaliation from a much bigger fish!).

3. Yes, schools have to set an example at times. A Y7 takes a knife into school. It is seen by his classmates. The school doesn't really have a choice but to exclude him in order that a message is clearly sent to all pupils that knives are not acceptable.

4. If your child was on the other end of the incident what would you be demanding happens?

5. Schools can be petty, and some staff hold grudges. A bit like any workplace. No, we are not supposed to, but we are human...well most of us!

6. Double standards exist (just as they do throughout life!) This is the equalities act at work. Some children will be allowed additional chances because of their protected characteristics. So, neurotypical Nell might be permanently excluded for thumping the TA whereas ASD/ADHD Tom gets a 5-day exclusion. Nell's family may feel this is unfair, but unfortunately Tom's disability means that reasonable adjustments have to be made.

7. Sometimes an exclusion is the best thing that can happen to a child.

- Access to additional support
- Assessment
- A fresh start
- Realisation they were on the wrong path

8. Where relationships have broken down you might not want a reinstatement, but you should still appeal if things were dealt with incorrectly. At this point in time you probably couldn't give two hoots about someone else's child, but it is important that if processes are not followed you do appeal in order to protect anything in the future.

9. Persistent disruption shouldn't exist and where it does, needs are not being met, or the

school is not the right environment. Maybe I'm biased. As a SENCO if I know a child is persistently disrupting learning, then I would want to know why and put measures in place to change things.

10. A PRU is a short-term placement and should never be seen as the 'next school'.

11. 45 days of fixed term exclusions is far too many. 15 days is sufficient to say that something isn't right.

12. Where a child has had a permanent exclusion, I personally feel, that a full assessment of needs is required with the possibility of an EHC Plan being issued. I'd be quite happy for them to have a different name and be limited to 3-years.

13. Schools that take on students who have been permanently excluded should be funded to support those students. Even if it's in the same way as Pupil Premium funding...after all, these children are no different to any other disadvantaged group or service children who have to move schools and make friends. Again, I'd happily accept it is only for an interim period of, let's say, 3-years. Why 3-years? Because the majority of students are permanently excluded in Y9. 3-years would take them to the end of GCSEs. Where a child is younger and needs it for longer than 3-years then they have a true EHCP need anyway!

14. I work with many schools, lots of whom have issues with knives. Knives are dangerous! That's why they appear in this list twice. Excluding a child with a knife is a suitable response. Permanent exclusions are the most common – why? To demonstrate to the rest of the school community that their safety is taken seriously. A managed move could be considered. It will depend on the reason WHY the child bought the knife into school.

I suspect along with never being Headteacher, I won't make Minister for Education either!

FAQ

My child has just been involved in an incident.
The school have just phoned.

1. **Can they insist I collect my child?**
   No. But...

   a. You might want to consider how your child is. If they have just been involved in an incident, then they probably need to leave the site to calm down. You would want to be there for them.

   b. If they normally travel to and from school on public transport or walk alone, then the school can release them. They do not need to 'retain' them until you get there.

   c. It MUST be recorded as an EXCLUSION.

   SEE [Processes] & [Duty of Care]

2. **They've suggested a part-time timetable. Do I have to agree?**
   No. But sometimes it suits everyone and allows your child to be successful for the time that they are in school and avoid an exclusion.
   It should be regularly reviewed with the intention of building up to fulltime as quickly as feasible
   Any non-school time is an AUTHORISED ABSENCE

   SEE [Part-time Timetable]

3. **They want to send my child home for lunch – can they do this?**
   Yes. It MUST be recorded as a HALF-DAY EXCLUSION for reporting purposes and 30 lunchtime exclusions in a term should trigger a governor's meeting. Be careful not to agree that your child is "coming home for lunch" which would not be recorded as an exclusion, removes your right to complain and is effectively hidden from the governors (and unlawful if being 'suggested'.)
   SEE [Fixed-Term Exclusions]

4. **School said he can't go to them and they've arranged for him to go to another**

provision for 6 weeks. Do I have to agree?
The school do not need your permission. If you object, then it is likely your child will be excluded. The school is taking reasonable steps to avoid this. You are responsible for transport there and back but often the school will offer support.

SEE [Alternative Provision]

5. **Can school force my child to attend a PRU?**
   No. PRUs are used generally for permanently excluded students but some schools are able to access their knowledge and expertise for students at risk of exclusion with short-term placements. You don't have to agree but you need to recognise that your child is at risk of permanent exclusion and the school is offering a model of support.

   SEE [Alternative Provision] + [PRU]

6. **School have said they want my child to try a managed move. Does he have to?**
   No. But as already suggested, if your child is at risk of exclusion this could help to avoid it. They are fresh starts and generally very successful.

   SEE [Managed Moves]

7. **The phone call was from the Head of Year. Does that mean it's not really an exclusion?**
   No. It is likely that someone you know will make the call. However, the decision will have been taken by the headteacher (or in their absence their designated deputy)

   SEE [Who Can Exclude]

8. **The incident happened on the way to school. Why are the school getting involved?**
   The school will have a behaviour policy that covers this. Whilst your child is travelling to and from school, they are also wearing their uniform and therefore the school could argue they are being bought into disrepute.

   SEE [Behaviour Policy] + [It happened outside school]

9. **School changed their mind. They've cancelled the exclusion can they do this?**

Yes. Provided it hasn't gone to the governors' board as an appeal, they can change their mind up to the last minute.

SEE [Governors]

10. **I don't think the exclusion is right or fair. Can I complain?**
Yes, but you need to make sure you follow the complaints policy exactly as it is set out. No trying to jump over heads.

SEE [Complaints]

11. **My child is due to sit public exams/SATS. Can they still do them?**
This is a decision that is entirely up to the school.

SEE [Exams]

12. **Is anyone protected from exclusion? My child is looked after/has an EHCP. School can't exclude them, can they?**
Yes. No one is exempt from exclusion. Reasonable adjustments should be made and where possible schools will try to avoid an exclusion, but no one has a magic cloak of protection.

SEE [EHCP] + [LAC] + [Vulnerable groups]

13. **I think my child has a special educational need.**
At the earliest opportunity speak to the school SENCO. Make sure you raise this at an appeal if you attend.

SEE [Special Educational Needs]

14. **School have said that they are going to extend the exclusion/convert it to a permanent one.**
Quite simply they can't. They can issue another exclusion to run immediately after this one finished in light of new evidence.

SEE [Conversion + Extension]

15. **I was rude to the school. I might have sworn and hit the Headteacher a little bit. Now they say my child can't come to their school.**
Oops! Your actions are not permitted to reflect on your child. They cannot exclude your child or ask you to move them to another school. They can, however, make

your life difficult!

SEE [You cannot be excluded for]

16. **I have work tomorrow. Its inconvenient for my child to be excluded.**
    Quite simply, tough. (Sorry, I say it like it is!)

    SEE [Parental Responsibility]

17. **Does a reintegration meeting have to take place?**
    No. It's good practice but not compulsory. If you can't attend an arranged meeting, then the exclusion cannot be extended.

    SEE [Reintegration]

18. **What information should the school give me?**
    The school should provide you with the exclusions letter, this should have in it all the information that you need.

    SEE [The Letter]

19. **Is there a limit on the number of exclusions?**
    Yes. A child can be excluded for up to 45 days in an academic year. Their school history follows them from one school to the next. So, further exclusions in a new school will be added on to their current total. This means they could end up in front of the governors if the 'fresh start' is not suitably used.
    There are trigger points and 15 days exclusion in a single term can lead to consideration of permanent exclusion.

    SEE [Fixed-term Exclusions]

20. **What happens to my child's education?**
    With a fixed-term exclusion your child will usually be provided with work to complete. For a permanent exclusion there will be information on the letter provided about what happens next. Most children will move to a PRU for a period of time before being placed in a new school.

    SEE [An education]

21. **Do school have any other choices?**
    Yes, schools have lots of choice and exclusion is the last resort most of the time.

The school also has alternative to exclusion, but they are not obliged to use them.

SEE [Alternatives]

22. **Who will know my child has been excluded?**
    I had a parent ask this as they were concerned that EVERYONE would know their son had been excluded. It is a difficult question to answer and it will depend on the school and the nature of the exclusion. For a fixed-term exclusion the class teachers are likely to be aware as the register tends to be pre-marked with the E. Any witnesses to the event tend to be aware. The last school I worked in had a staff briefing every other morning, and any students who were returning from an exclusion were flagged in the meeting so we could be aware. Whilst I understand the reluctance for everyone to know about the exclusion, it can actually be a useful piece of information. (From why they didn't do the last piece of homework, to providing extra support to catch up with any missed work or ensuring that they are sat away from any distractions or issues.) If schools are to work with the child to avoid further exclusions then changes often need to be made, perhaps to seating plans, or expectations in lessons. Without being informed of this there develops a system whereby the child is doomed to fail again as nothing changes.

    SEE [Early Help] + [Reintegration] + [PSP]

REAL EXAMPLES

My 15-year-old son is on a managed move. He is awaiting assessment of ADHD/ASD. He lost his temper over some silly thing. He trashed the room (tables, whiteboard, walls) and injured himself. I suspect he will be taken off his managed move and permanently excluded.

My response: It really will depend on the school. He can't be permanently excluded in response to his original reason for being on the managed move. However, they may consider that the placement has broken down and that an exclusion for this new 'offence' is required. If the host school had been fully informed about the possible ADHD/ASD and the reasons behind the original managed move, then they hadn't put everything in place to support him and avoid him losing his temper. On the other hand, if they hadn't been fully informed by his home school then they have been neglectful and a firmly worded letter when presenting your case to the governors may help any exclusion to be overturned.

My 5-year-old has suspected ASD/ADHD. He's been permanently excluded. I appealed because the school didn't follow their procedures. The HT changed their mind 2 hours before the meeting.

My response: This is a perfectly acceptable response by headteacher. A little bit annoying, but they have obviously recognised that they made a mistake in their procedures and that their governing body have a strong moral compass that was going to fall on the correct side of the law. They have chosen to repeal the permanent exclusion and therefore this will not sit on your child's record.

I was called to collect my child during a meltdown. I was not told it would be an exclusion. I've had no contact, so I emailed the school and met the SENCO. She didn't mention an exclusion. On the way out I was handed an exclusion letter (½ day) with the wrong dates. My son has not been asked for his views.

My response: There are several things wrong here.
1. If you are asked to collect your child and it is not an exclusion, what were they intending to mark it down as? Always ask if you are asked to collect your child early how it will be recorded in the register. You are being asked to take them home therefore it is an exclusion. (Remember, I sit on the fence here as I could argue it is medical.)
2. If you thought it wasn't an exclusion, I'm not sure why you didn't just send them in as normal the following day, instead you were waiting for them to make contact. This seems a little unusual.
3. Meeting the SENCO was a good idea, but unless they are your child's class teacher, they

might not have all the information about the event. You clarified in another post that you hadn't told the SENCO why you were coming in and that the SENCO only works 1 day a week at your school.

4. The letter can be handed to you although I would have handed it straight back to the school if it had the incorrect dates on it. There seems to be a degree of confusion for everyone concerned.

5. Your son was in the middle of a meltdown when you collected him, he was unable to give his views. You then kept him off school and he hasn't been in since – when do you expect the school to collect his views?

This parent was obviously frustrated and probably didn't give enough detail on Facebook for their post to make much sense, but actually, their behaviour made it much more difficult for the school to do what they were required to do.

I've been given a £60 bill for 2 canvas prints. I've been told to pay, or the school will involve the police and youth offending team. He's done an internal 2-day exclusion.

My response: This is vandalism. Schools do have insurance, but for something at £60 their excess would be higher than this. (The canvas prints were produced by students of the school for their A-level Art exam, students have to buy their own canvases and these students should not be out of pocket because of your child's behaviour.) Yes, the school can involve the police and YOT, they're trying to avoid that for you and giving your son a chance to 'pay' for his mistake.

School have been asking me to collect my son each afternoon (about 2 pm). They've said it won't go down as an exclusion.

My response: This is unlawful. If the school is not providing your child with a fulltime education and you have not agreed to a part-time provision, then they are illegally excluding your child. You have two options. 1. Refuse to collect him. 2. Request that they are recorded as exclusions (after 2 weeks they will have to report to their own governing body.) Remember that unless they are recorded as exclusions you cannot bring forth a complaint about your child being 'excluded'.

Why did the school not exclude my son?

My eldest son has inherited my ability to ask the most awkward questions at the most awkward times. It is scary how I hear my own voice when he speaks. He was challenging of a member of staff in school, using his knowledge of school policies and procedures and DfE guidance to challenge something the teacher had said. To be fair, he was in the right, unfortunately, his attitude stinks! The member of staff didn't like the way he was spoken to (or the fact that he had proved them wrong) and gave my son a 30-minute detention (school calls them 'work recovery sessions') after school the following day. As my son has to collect his younger brother from school, this wasn't an option and I wrote this on the reply slip. I also took the opportunity to point out that there was no 'work to recover' since he was being penalised for his opinion and attitude. Don't get me wrong, I'd, personally, love to buy and use a bar of carbolic soap on many occasions, and I would have accepted him having to apologise to the member of staff or sit the detention over a break or lunch. School were not accommodating. They simply stated if he didn't attend that detention it would double to 1 hour, then to 2 hours on a Friday and finally would end up as being a day in the isolation room with a view to a fixed-term exclusion if he didn't do this. They took great care to send me this on letter headed paper. I simply printed out a copy of their (out of date) behaviour policy, attached it to the letter and asked them to highlight exactly which rule he had broken and the 'tariff' relevant to this along with indicating exactly where in their policy this 'doubling' of detentions was mentioned. School replied that their new policy hadn't been ratified by the governors and they didn't have a copy to share with me. I'm sure by now, you will realise that this just caused me to laugh and send back a reply stating that the school was not able to operate a policy that their governors had not ratified or that parents and students were unaware of. I also pointed out that the inspectors (the school is in special measures) would love to analyse the piece of data around a child receiving a fixed-term exclusion for 'correcting a staff member'. Six months later and the school still haven't ratified the 'new' behaviour policy...and no one has tried to chase my son for his detention or the exclusion.

The irony of the tale is that my son was correcting the member of staff with regards to their support of an exclusion to a student who had recognised special educational needs that caused them to tic and 'throw' what was in their hands at the time! They had thrown a pen which hit a teacher and received an exclusion. (I have a potential special needs lawyer in the house...)

HELP

- IPSEA: https://www.ipsea.org.uk

- Special needs jungle: https://specialneedsjungle.com

- Just for kids' law: http://justforkidslaw.org

- Ambitious about autism: https://www.ambitiousaboutautism.org.uk

- Education rights alliance: http://educationalrightsalliance.blogspot.com

- National parents partnership network: https://councilfordisabledchildren.org.uk/information-advice-and-support-services-network

- Coram children's legal centre: https://www.childrenslegalcentre.com

- Communities empowerment network: http://cenlive.org

- Children's commissioner: https://www.childrenscommissioner.gov.uk

- UCL access to justice: https://www.ucl.ac.uk/access-to-justice/

- ACE education: http://www.ace-ed.org.uk

- Behaviour teach:

- The School Exclusions Project – www.theschoolexclusionproject.com. This group provide free legal representation to challenge permanent exclusions. The volunteers are supervised by City University and Matrix Chambers and will represent at all stages specialising in cases involving SEN.

- SENDIAS: Look on your local authority website under Local Offer for details of the special educational needs and disability support available in your area.

Appendix

School Exclusion – The Parent Guide

Sample Letter for a fixed-term exclusion

Letter 1: Fixed period exclusions of a 5 school days or fewer (cumulative total in one term) and where a public examination is not missed.

Dear [Parent's Name]

I am writing to inform you of my decision to exclude [Child's Name] for a fixed period of [specify period]. The exclusion begins/began on [date] and ends on [date]. I realise that this period may well be upsetting for [Child's Name], you and your family, but the decision to exclude [Child's Name] has not been taken lightly. [Child's Name] has been excluded for this fixed period because [reason for exclusion].

Since your child is of compulsory school age, you have a duty to ensure that your child is not present in a public place during school hours for the duration of this exclusion [specify dates] unless there is reasonable justification for this. I must inform you that you may be prosecuted or receive a fixed penalty notice from the local authority if your child is present in a public place during school hours on the specified dates. It will be for you to show that there is reasonable justification.

We will set work for [Child's Name] to be completed on the days specified in the previous paragraph as school days during the period of his/her exclusion [detail the arrangements for this]. Please ensure that work set by the school is completed and returned to us promptly for marking.

You have the right to make representations about this decision to the governing board. If you wish to make representations please contact the clerk to governors [Name of Contact] on/at [contact details – address, phone number, email], as soon as possible. Whilst the governing board has no power to direct reinstatement, they must consider any representations you make and may place a copy of their findings on your child's school record.

You should also be aware that if you think the exclusion occurred as a result of discrimination, you can make a claim under the Equality Act 2010 to the First Tier Tribunal (Special Educational Needs and Disability) in the case of disability discrimination, or the County Court in the case of other forms of discrimination. If you wish to make a claim of discrimination, please be aware that such a claim must be lodged within six months of the date in which the discrimination is alleged to have taken place.

Information on disability discrimination and other forms of discrimination claims are available on the HM Courts and Tribunal Service website at:

http://www.justice.gov.uk/tribunals/send

Making a claim would not affect your right to make representations to the governing board.

You also have the right to see a copy of [Child's Name]'s school record. Due to confidentiality restrictions, you will need to notify me in writing if you wish to be supplied with a copy of [Child's Name]'s school record. I will be happy to supply you with a copy if you request it. There may be a charge for photocopying.

You may wish to contact for advice and information, ▇▇, at Local Authority at ▇▇.

The Department for Education (DfE) have developed exclusion guidance for parents which can be accessed via the following web links:

http://www.gov.uk/school-discipline-exclusions/exclusions
http://www.gov.uk/government/publications/school-exclusion

You may also find it useful to contact ▇▇ Information, Advice and Support Service for SEND (formerly Parent Partnership), a local organisation that can offer exclusion support. They can be contacted at ias.service@▇▇.gov.uk or ▇▇. Alternatively, other useful contacts that provide impartial advice and information to parents on education matters include:

- The Coram Children's Legal Centre – www.childrenslegalcentre.com
- ACE Education – http://www.ace-ed.org.uk or 0300 011 5142
- Independent Parental Special Education Advice – http://www.ipsea.org.uk/
- The National Autistic Society (NAS) School Exclusion Service (England) – schoolexclusions@nas.org.uk or 0808 800 4002

[Child's Name]'s exclusion expires on [date] and we expect [Child's Name] to be back in school on [date] at [time].

Yours sincerely ▇

[Name] Head teacher

Sample letter for a permanent exclusion

Letter 4 - Permanent exclusion notification letter.

Dear [Parent's Name]

I regret to inform you of my decision to permanently exclude [Child's Name] with effect from [date]. This means that [Child's Name] will not be allowed in the school unless he/she is reinstated by the governing board. I realise that this exclusion may well be upsetting for [Child's Name], you and your family, but the decision to permanently exclude [Child's Name] has not been taken lightly. [Child's Name] has been excluded because [reasons for the exclusion — include any other relevant previous history].

Since your child is of compulsory school age you have a duty to ensure that your child is not present in a public place during school hours for the duration of the first 5 school days of this exclusion, i.e. on [specify the precise dates] unless there is reasonable justification for this. I must inform you that you could be prosecuted or receive a penalty notice if your child is present in a public place during school hours on those dates. It will be for you to show that there is reasonable justification.

Alternative arrangements for [Child's Name]'s education to continue will be made. For the first five school days of the exclusion we will set work for [Child's Name] and would ask you to ensure this work is completed and returned promptly to school for marking. From the sixth school day of the exclusion onwards — i.e. from [specify the date] the local authority [give the name of the authority in which the family reside] will provide suitable full-time education [choose one of the following options]:

- For ▆▆▆ residents only - arrangements for full-time education will be organised by the ▆▆▆ who can be contacted on ▆▆▆
- For non-▆▆▆ residents - I have also today informed [name of officer] at [name of local authority] of your child's exclusion and they will be in touch with you about arrangements for [his/her] education from the sixth school day of exclusion. You can contact them at [give contact details].

As this is a permanent exclusion the governing board must meet to consider it. At the meeting you may make representations to the governing board if you wish and ask them to reinstate your child in school. The governing board has the power to reinstate your child immediately or from a specified date, or alternatively, they have the power to uphold the exclusion in which case you may have the decision reviewed by an Independent Review Panel. The latest date by which the governing board must meet is [specify the date — the 15th school day after the date on which the governing board was notified of the exclusion]. If you wish to make representations to the governing board and wish to be accompanied by a friend or representative, at your own expense, please contact clerk to governors [name of contact] on/at [contact details — address, phone number, email], as soon as possible.

Your child may also be involved in this meeting to speak on his/her own behalf if it is appropriate, taking into account his/her age and level of understanding. You will, whether you choose to make representations or not, be notified by the clerk to the governing board of the time, date and location of the meeting. Please let us know if you have a disability or special needs so that suitable arrangements may be made for you to attend the meeting at

school. Also, please inform [above contact] if it would be helpful for you to have an interpreter present at the meeting.

You should also be aware that if you think the exclusion occurred as a result of discrimination, you can make a claim under the Equality Act 2010 to the First Tier Tribunal (Special Educational Needs and Disability) in the case of disability discrimination, or the County Court in the case of other forms of discrimination. If you wish to make a claim of discrimination, please be aware that such a claim must be lodged within six months of the date in which the discrimination is alleged to have taken place.

Information on disability discrimination and other forms of discrimination claims are available on the HM Courts and Tribunal Service website at:

http://www.justice.gov.uk/tribunals/send

Making a claim would not affect your right to make representations to the governing board.

You have the right to see a copy of [Name of Child]'s school record. Due to confidentiality restrictions, you must notify me in writing if you wish to be supplied with a copy of [Name of Child]'s school record. I will be happy to supply you with a copy if you request it. There may be a charge for photocopying.

You may wish to contact for advice and information, ▆▆▆ at ▆▆▆ or ▆▆▆ LA at ▆▆▆

The Department for Education (DfE) have developed exclusion guidance for parents which can be accessed via the following web links.

http://www.gov.uk/school-discipline-exclusions/exclusions
http://www.gov.uk/government/publications/school-exclusion

You may also find it useful to contact ▆▆▆ Information, Advice and Support Service for SEND (formerly Parent Partnership), a local organisation that can offer exclusion support. They can be contacted at as service@▆▆▆ gov.uk or ▆▆▆. Alternatively, other useful contacts that provide impartial advice and information to parents on education matters include:

- The Coram Children's Legal Centre – www.childrenslegalcentre.com
- ACE Education – http://www.ace-ed.org.uk or 0300 011 5142
- Independent Parental Special Education Advice – http://www.ipsea.org.uk/
- The National Autistic Society (NAS) School Exclusion Service (England) – schoolexclusions@nas.org.uk or 0808 800 4002

Yours sincerely

[Name] Head teacher

School Exclusion – The Parent Guide

Sample letter from a governing body upholding an appealed exclusion

Letter 5 - Permanent exclusion – governing board upheld decision letter.

Dear [Parent's name]

The meeting of the governing board at [school's name] on [date] considered the decision by [head teacher] to permanently exclude your son/daughter [name of pupil]. The governing board, after carefully considering both the oral and written representations made by you and the head teacher, and all the available evidence, has decided to uphold [Child's name]'s exclusion.

The reasons for the governing board's decision are as follows: [give the reasons in as much detail as possible, explaining how they were arrived at.]

You have the right to have the decision of the governing board reviewed by an independent review panel. You must set out the reasons for wanting the review in your application and include any written evidence you wish to submit. If appropriate, you may also include reference to any special educational needs that your child has that is relevant to this exclusion.

If you would like to request a review, please apply in writing to [choose one of the following options]:

- Maintained schools only –
- Academies – provide alternative contact details for the substitute contact deemed appropriate by your academy trust

The request for review must be received by [Democratic Services/Academies' contact], no later than the 15th school day after parental receipt of this letter]. If you have not lodged an application by [repeat latest date], you will lose your right to have the decision to exclude your child reviewed by an independent review panel. Please advise if you have a disability or special needs so that suitable arrangements may be made for you to attend the review hearing. Also, please inform [name of the contact listed above] if it would be helpful for you to have an interpreter present at the review hearing. You can have someone to make written and/or oral representations to the Independent Review Panel on your behalf and at your own expense. You may also wish to bring a friend with you to the review hearing.

Irrespective of whether the school regards your child as having special educational needs, you are entitled to have a Special Educational Needs (SEN) expert at the review hearing. The role of the SEN expert is to provide impartial specialist advice to the panel on how special educational needs might be relevant to the exclusion, but does not include making an assessment of your child's special educational needs. The SEN expert's advice will focus on whether the school's policies which relate to SEN, or the application of these policies in relation to this case, were lawful, reasonable and procedurally fair. If you wish to have a SEN expert at the review hearing, please clearly indicate this on your application and be aware that the cost of appointment of the SEN expert will be met by the local authority (if maintained school) or Academy Trust (if academy) [amend as appropriate].

Your review hearing will be heard by an independent review panel. A three-member panel will comprise:- one serving, or recently retired (within the last five years), head teacher, one serving, or recently serving, experienced governor/ management committee member, and one lay member who will be the Chairman

[Use the following paragraph only if there is a possibility that a five-member panel may sit]

[A five-member panel will comprise - two serving, or recently retired (within the last 5 years), head teachers; two serving, experienced governors / management committee members and one lay member who will be the Chairman.]

The review panel will rehear all the facts of the case – if you have fresh evidence to present to the panel you may do so. The panel must meet no later than the 15th school day after the date on which your application for a review is lodged. In exceptional circumstances panels may adjourn the review hearing until a later date.

In reviewing the governing board's decision to exclude, the panel can make one of three decisions:

i. they may uphold your child's exclusion;

ii. they may recommend that the governing board reconsiders their decision, or

iii. quash the decision and direct that the governing board considers the exclusion again.

In addition to your right to apply for an independent review hearing, if you believe that the exclusion occurred as a result of discrimination, you can make a claim under the Equality Act 2010 to the First Tier Tribunal (Special Educational Needs and Disability) in the case of disability discrimination, or the County Court in the case of other forms of discrimination. If you would like to make a claim of discrimination, please be aware that such a claim must be lodged within six months of the date in which the discrimination is alleged to have taken place.

Information on disability discrimination and other forms of discrimination claims are available on the HM Courts and Tribunal Service website at:

http://www.justice.gov.uk/tribunals/send

The Department for Education (DfE) have developed exclusion guidance for parents which can be accessed via the following web links:

http://www.gov.uk/school-discipline-exclusions/exclusions
http://www.gov.uk/government/publications/school-exclusion

You may also find it useful to contact ▓▓▓▓ Information, Advice and Support Service for SEND (formerly Parent Partnership), a local organisation that can offer exclusion support. They can be contacted at ias.service@▓▓▓▓.gov.uk or ▓▓▓▓. Alternatively, other useful contacts that provide impartial advice and information to parents on education matters include:

- The Coram Children's Legal Centre – www.childrenslegalcentre.com
- ACE Education – http://www.ace-ed.org.uk or 0300 0115142
- Independent Parental Special Education Advice – http://www.ipsea.org.uk/
- The National Autistic Society NAS) School Exclusion Service (England) – schoolexclusions@nas.org.uk or 0808 800 4002

The arrangements currently being made for [Child's name]'s education will continue. [Specify details here].

Yours sincerely

[name] [Clerk to the Governing Board]

Law:

Rules governing exclusions:

s52 Education Act 2002 http://www/legislation/gov.uk/ukpga/2002/32/section/52)

Exclusion of pupils

(1)The headteacher of a maintained school may exclude a pupil from the school for a fixed period or permanently.
(2)The teacher in charge of a pupil referral unit may exclude a pupil from the unit for a fixed period or permanently.
(3)Regulations shall make provision—
(a)requiring prescribed persons to be given prescribed information relating to any exclusion under subsection (1) or (2),
(b)requiring the responsible body, in prescribed cases, to consider whether the pupil should be reinstated,
(c)requiring the local education authority to make arrangements for enabling a prescribed person to appeal, in any prescribed case, to a panel constituted in accordance with the regulations against any decision of the responsible body not to reinstate a pupil, and
(d)as to the procedure on appeals.
(4)Regulations under this section may also make provision—
(a)for the payment by the local education authority of allowances to members of a panel constituted in accordance with the regulations,
(b)requiring a person or body exercising functions under subsection (1) or (2) or under the regulations to have regard to any guidance given from time to time (in relation to England) by the Secretary of State or (in relation to Wales) by the National Assembly for Wales,
(c)requiring local education authorities to give prescribed information to the Secretary of State or the Assembly, as the case may be, and
(d)in relation to any other matter relating to the exercise of the powers conferred by subsections (1) and (2).
(5)In subsection (3), "the responsible body" means—
(a)in relation to exclusion from a maintained school, the governing body of the school, and
(b)in relation to exclusion from a pupil referral unit, such person as may be prescribed;
and, in relation to any time when no responsible body is prescribed in relation to permanent exclusion from a pupil referral unit, subsection (3) shall have effect in relation to such an exclusion with the omission of paragraph (b) and as if the decision referred to in paragraph (c) were the decision of the teacher in charge of the unit permanently to exclude the pupil.
(6)Regulations made by virtue of subsection (4)(a) may provide for any of the provisions of sections 173 to 174 of the Local Government Act 1972 (c. 70) (allowances to members of local authorities and other bodies) to apply with prescribed modifications in relation to members of a panel constituted in accordance with regulations under this section.
(7)Regulations shall make provision enabling a prescribed person, in any prescribed case, to appeal to a panel constituted in accordance with the regulations against any decision made after 31st August 1994 under paragraph 7 of Schedule 1 to the Education Act 1996 (c. 56), or any enactment repealed by that Act, in relation to the permanent exclusion of a pupil from a pupil referral unit; and the provision that may be made by regulations made by virtue of this subsection in relation to any such decision includes any provision that could after the commencement of subsections (2) to (4) be made in relation to a decision falling within subsection (3)(c).
(8)Regulations under this section which—
(a)relate to exclusions from pupil referral units (whether before or after the passing of this Act), and

(b)are made before the repeal by this Act of the existing enactments is fully in force,
may provide for any provision made by or under the existing enactments to have effect in relation to exclusions from pupil referral units with such modifications as may be prescribed.
(9)In subsection (8) "the existing enactments" means sections 64(2) and (3) and 65 to 67 of, and Schedule 18 to, the School Standards and Framework Act 1998 (c. 31).
(10)In this section "exclude", in relation to the exclusion of a child from a school or pupil referral unit, means exclude on disciplinary grounds (and "exclusion" shall be construed accordingly).
(11)In this section "maintained school" has the same meaning as in Chapter 1.

Equalities Act

Equality Act 2010 http://www.legislation.gov.uk/ukpga/2010/15/contents

Provision of a full-time education

S100 Educations and Inspections Act 2006 - http://www.legislation.gov.uk/ukpga/2006/40/section/100

Duty of governing body or proprietor where pupil excluded for fixed period
(1)Except in prescribed cases, the governing body of a relevant school in England must make arrangements for the provision of suitable full-time education for pupils of compulsory school age who are excluded from the school for a fixed period on disciplinary grounds.
(2)The education referred to in subsection (1) must be provided from a day that, in relation to the pupil concerned, is determined in accordance with regulations.
(3)The education must not be provided at the school unless it is provided there in pursuance of arrangements which—
(a)are made jointly with the governing body of at least one other relevant school, and
(b)make provision for the education of pupils excluded on disciplinary grounds from any of the schools that are parties to the arrangements.
(4)In determining what arrangements to make under subsection (1) in the case of any pupil, a governing body must have regard to any guidance given from time to time by the Secretary of State.
(5)In this section—
"governing body", in relation to a relevant school which is an Academy, a city technology college or a city college for the technology of the arts, means proprietor;
"prescribed" means prescribed by regulations;
"regulations" means regulations made by the Secretary of State;
"relevant school" does not include a pupil referral unit;
"suitable full-time education", in relation to a pupil, means efficient full-time education suitable to his age, ability and aptitude and to any special educational needs he may have.

http://www.legislation.gov.uk/ukpga/1996/56/section/19

Exceptional provision of education in pupil referral units or elsewhere.

(1) Each [F1local authority] shall make arrangements for the provision of suitable F2. . . education at school or otherwise than at school for those children of compulsory school age who, by reason of illness, exclusion from school or otherwise, may not for any period receive suitable education unless such arrangements are made for them.
[F3(1A) In relation to England, subsection (1) does not apply in the case of a child—
(a) who will cease to be of compulsory school age within the next six weeks, and
(b) does not have any relevant examinations to complete.
In paragraph (b) "relevant examinations" means any public examinations or other assessments for which the child has been entered.]
(2) Any school established (whether before or after the commencement of this Act) and maintained by a [F1local authority] which—
(a) is specially organised to provide education for such children, and
(b) is not a county school or a special school,
shall be known as a "pupil referral unit".
[F4(2A) Subsection (2) does not apply in relation to schools in England.
(2B)(2B) Any school established in England (whether before or after the commencement of this Act) and maintained by a [F1local authority] which—
(a) is specially organised to provide education for such children, and
(b) is not a community or foundation school, a community or foundation special school, or a maintained nursery school,
shall be known as a "pupil referral unit".]
(3) A [F1local authority] may secure the provision of boarding accommodation at any pupil referral unit.
[F5[F6(3A) In relation to England, the education to be provided for a child in pursuance of arrangements made by a local authority under subsection (1) shall be—
(a) full-time education, or
(b) in the case of a child within subsection (3AA), education on such part-time basis as the authority consider to be in the child's best interests.
(3AA) A child is within this subsection if the local authority considers that, for reasons which relate to the physical or mental health of the child, it would not be in the child's best interests for full-time education to be provided for the child.]
(3B)[F7Regulations may provide that the education to be provided for a child in pursuance of arrangements made by a local authority in England under subsection (1)] must be provided from a day that, in relation to the pupil concerned, is determined in accordance with [F8the regulations] .]
(4) A [F1local authority] may make arrangements for the provision of suitable F2. . . education otherwise than at school for those young persons who, by reason of illness, exclusion from school or otherwise, may not for any period receive suitable education unless such arrangements are made for them.
[F9(4A) In determining what arrangements to make under subsection (1) or (4) in the case of any child or young person a [F1local authority] shall have regard to any guidance given from time to time by the Secretary of State.]
(5) Any child for whom education is provided otherwise than at school in pursuance of this section, and any young person for whom full-time education is so provided in pursuance of this section, shall be treated for the purposes of this Act as a pupil.
[F10(6) In this section—
- "relevant school" means—

(a) a maintained school,

(b) an Academy,

(c) a city technology college, or

(d) a city college for the technology of the arts;

- "suitable education", in relation to a child or young person, means efficient education suitable to his age, ability and aptitude and to any special educational needs he may have (and "suitable full-time education" is to be read accordingly).]

(7) Schedule 1 has effect in relation to pupil referral units.

Exclusion from maintained schools, academies and pupil referral units in England

Summary

This document from the Department for Education provides a guide to the legislation that governs the exclusion of pupils from maintained schools, pupil referral units (PRUs), academy schools (including free schools, studio schools and university technology colleges) and alternative provision academies (including alternative provision free schools) in England.

The 'guide to the law' sections in this guidance should not be used as a substitute for legislation and legal advice.

The document also provides statutory guidance to which headteacherrs, governing boards, local authorities, academy trusts, independent review panel members and special educational needs (SEN) experts must have regard when carrying out their functions in relation to exclusions. Clerks to independent review panels must also be trained to know and understand this guidance.

The phrase 'must have regard', when used in this context, does not mean that the sections of statutory guidance have to be followed in every detail, but that they should be followed unless there is a good reason not to in a particular case.

Where relevant, this document refers to other guidance in areas such as behaviour, SEN, and equality, but it is not intended to provide detailed guidance on these issues.

This document replaces the version published in 2012 for schools in England.

Expiry or review date

This guidance will be kept under review and updated as necessary.

Who is this publication for?

This guidance is for:

Headteachers, governing boards, local authorities, academy trusts, independent review panel members, independent review panel clerks, and individuals appointed as SEN experts.

The term 'head teacher' in this document includes the teacher in charge at a PRU and principals of academies.

The term 'governing board' includes the governing body of a maintained school, the management committee of a PRU and the academy trust of an academy. Except where specifically stated, this guide applies to all maintained schools, academy schools (including free schools but not 16-19 academies), alternative provision academies (including alternative provision free schools), and PRUs. The term 'school' in this document is used to describe any school to which the guidance applies. Where the term 'academy' is used it refers to any category of academy to which the guidance applies.

Except in relation to pupils in PRUs, or where stated, the requirements of the guide apply in relation to all pupils, including those who may be below or above compulsory school age, such as those attending nursery classes or sixth forms.

This guide does not apply to independent schools (other than the academies listed above), city technology colleges, city colleges for the technology of the arts, sixth form colleges or 16-19 academies, all of which have separate exclusion procedures. Local authorities are, however, required to arrange educational provision for pupils of compulsory school age who are excluded from these institutions if they would not otherwise receive such education.

About this guide

What legislation does this guide relate to?

The principal legislation to which this guidance relates is:

the Education Act 2002, as amended by the Education Act 2011;

the School Discipline (Pupil Exclusions and Reviews) (England) Regulations 2012;

the Education and Inspections Act 2006;

the Education Act 1996; and

the Education (Provision of Full-Time Education for Excluded Pupils) (England) Regulations 2007, as amended by the Education (Provision of Full-Time Education for Excluded Pupils) (England) (Amendment) Regulations 2014.

Definition of 'parents' in this guidance

The definition of a parent for the purposes of the Education Acts is broadly drawn. In addition to the child's birth parents, references to parents in this guidance include any person who has parental responsibility (which includes the local authority where it has a care order in respect of the child) and any person (for example, a foster carer) with whom the child lives. Where practicable, all those with parental responsibility should be involved in the exclusions process. (Further information for parents on exclusion can be found in Annex C to this guidance entitled *a guide for parents/carers*).

Legislation on exclusion gives clarity and certainty to schools, local authorities, academy trusts and review panels, in terms of how they discharge their obligations to parents. Obligations are to the 'relevant person' – a parent or the pupil, aged 18 or over.

Definition of 'term' and 'academic year' in this guidance

Where a school's academic year consists of three terms or fewer, a reference to a 'term' in this guidance means one of those terms. Where a school's academic year consists of more than three terms, then a reference to 'term' means the periods from 31 December to Easter Monday, from Easter Monday to 31 July and from 31 July to 31 December.

In this guidance 'academic year' means a school's academic year beginning with the first day of school after 31 July and ending with the first day of school after the following 31 July.

Key points

The legislation governing the exclusion process remains unchanged. This statutory guidance has been updated in a small number of areas, in particular to provide greater confidence to head teachers on their use of exclusion and to provide greater clarity to independent review panels and governing boards on their consideration of exclusion decisions.

In January 2015, the Department amended regulations to clarify that a governing board's duty to arrange education from the sixth day of a fixed-period exclusion is triggered by consecutive fixed-period exclusions totalling more than five days[1].

Good discipline in schools is essential to ensure that all pupils can benefit from the opportunities provided by education. The Government supports head teachers in using exclusion as a sanction where it is warranted. However, permanent exclusion should only be used as a last resort, in response to a serious breach or persistent breaches of the school's behaviour policy; and where allowing the pupil to remain in school would seriously harm the education or welfare of the pupil or others in the school.

The decision to exclude a pupil must be lawful, reasonable and fair. Schools have a statutory duty not to discriminate against pupils on the basis of protected characteristics, such as disability or race. Schools should give particular consideration to the fair treatment of pupils from groups who are vulnerable to exclusion.

Disruptive behaviour can be an indication of unmet needs. Where a school has concerns about a pupil's behaviour, it should try to identify whether there are any causal factors and intervene early in order to reduce the need for a subsequent exclusion. In this situation, schools should consider whether a multi-agency assessment that goes beyond the pupil's educational needs is required.

Schools should have a strategy for reintegrating a pupil who returns to school following a fixed-period exclusion and for managing their future behaviour.

All children have a right to education. Schools should take reasonable steps to set and mark work for pupils during the first five school days of an exclusion; and alternative provision must be arranged from the sixth day. There are obvious benefits in arranging alternative provision to begin as soon as possible after an exclusion.

Where parents dispute the decision of a governing board not to reinstate a permanently excluded pupil, they can ask for this decision to be reviewed by an independent review panel. Where there is an allegation of discrimination (under the Equality Act 2010) in relation to a fixed-period or permanent exclusion, parents can also make a claim to the First-tier Tribunal (Special Educational Needs and Disability) for disability discrimination, or the County Court for other forms of discrimination.

An independent review panel does not have the power to direct a governing board to reinstate an excluded pupil. However, where a panel decides that a governing board's decision is flawed when considered in the light of the principles applicable on an application for judicial review, it can direct a governing board to reconsider its decision. The panel will then be expected to order that the school must make an additional payment of £4,000 if it does not offer to reinstate the pupil. Whether or not a school recognises a pupil as having SEN, all parents have the right to request the presence of an SEN expert at a review meeting. The SEN expert's role is to advise the review panel, orally or in writing or both, impartially, of the relevance of SEN in the context and circumstances of the review. For example, they may advise whether the school acted reasonably in relation to its legal duties when excluding the pupil.

Excluded pupils should be enabled and encouraged to participate at all stages of the exclusion process, taking into account their age and ability to understand

The head teacher's power to exclude

A guide to the law[2]

Only the head teacher[3] of a school can exclude a pupil and this must be on disciplinary grounds. A pupil may be excluded for one or more fixed periods (up to a maximum of 45 school days in a single academic year), or permanently. A fixed-period exclusion does not have to be for a continuous period. (Annex B of this guidance, *a non- statutory guide for head teachers*, summarises the requirements for head teachers, but should not be used as a substitute for this guidance or the relevant legislation.)

A fixed-period exclusion can also be for parts of the school day. For example, if a pupil's behaviour at lunchtime is disruptive, they may be excluded from the school premises for the duration of the lunchtime period. The legal requirements relating to exclusion, such as the head teacher's duty to notify parents, apply in all cases. Lunchtime exclusions are counted as half a school day for statistical purposes and in determining whether a governing board meeting is triggered.

The law does not allow for extending a fixed-period exclusion or 'converting' a fixed-period exclusion into a permanent exclusion. In exceptional cases, usually where further evidence has come to light, a further fixed-period exclusion may be issued to begin immediately after the first period ends; or a permanent exclusion may be issued to begin immediately after the end of the fixed period.

The behaviour of a pupil outside school can be considered grounds for an exclusion.

The head teacher may withdraw an exclusion that has not been reviewed by the governing board.

Any decision of a school, including exclusion, must be made in line with the principles of administrative law, i.e. that it is: lawful (with respect to the legislation relating directly to exclusions and a school's wider legal duties, including the European Convention on Human Rights and the Equality Act 2010); rational; reasonable; fair; and proportionate.

The head teacher must take account of their legal duty of care when sending a pupil home following an exclusion.

When establishing the facts in relation to an exclusion decision the head teacher must apply the civil standard of proof; i.e. 'on the balance of probabilities' it is more likely than not that a fact is true, rather than the criminal standard of 'beyond reasonable doubt.' This means that the head teacher should accept that something happened if it is more likely that it happened than that it did not happen.

Under the Equality Act 2010 (the Equality Act), schools must not discriminate against, harass or victimise pupils because of: sex; race; disability; religion or belief; sexual orientation; pregnancy/maternity; or gender reassignment. For disabled children, this includes a duty to make reasonable adjustments to policies and practices and the provision of auxiliary aids.

In carrying out their functions, the public sector equality duty means schools must also have due regard to the need to:

eliminate discrimination, harassment, victimisation, and other conduct that is prohibited by the Equality Act;

advance equality of opportunity between people who share a protected characteristic and people who do not; and foster good relations between people who share a protected characteristic and people who do not share it.

These duties need to be complied with when deciding whether to exclude a pupil. Schools must also ensure that their policies and practices do not discriminate against pupils by unfairly increasing their risk of exclusion. Provisions within the Equality Act allow schools to take positive action to deal with particular disadvantages, needs, or low participation affecting one group, where this can be shown to be a proportionate way of dealing with such issues[4].

The head teacher and governing board must comply with their statutory duties in relation to SEN when administering the exclusion process. This includes having regard to the SEND Code of Practice[5].

It is unlawful to exclude for a non-disciplinary reason. For example, it would be unlawful to exclude a pupil simply because they have additional needs or a disability that the school feels it is unable to meet, or for a reason such as: academic attainment/ability; the action of a pupil's parents; or the failure of a pupil to meet specific conditionsbefore they are reinstated, such as to attend a reintegration meeting. However, a pupil who repeatedly disobeys their teachers' academic instructions could, be subject to exclusion.

'Informal' or 'unofficial' exclusions, such as sending a pupil home 'to cool off', are unlawful, regardless of whether they occur with the agreement of parents or carers. Any exclusion of a pupil, even for short periods of time, must be formally recorded.

Maintained schools have the power to direct a pupil off-site for education to improve their behaviour[6]. A pupil at any type of school can also transfer to another school as part of a 'managed move' where this occurs with the consent of the parties involved, including the parents and the admission authority of the school. However, the threat of exclusion must never be used to influence parents to remove their child from theschool.

Statutory guidance on factors that a head teacher should take into account before taking the decision to exclude

A decision to exclude a pupil permanently should only be taken:

in response to a serious breach or persistent breaches of the school's behaviour policy; and

where allowing the pupil to remain in school would seriously harm the education or welfare of the pupil or others in the school.

The decision on whether to exclude is for the head teacher to take. However, where practical, the head teacher should give the pupil an opportunity to present their case before taking the decision to exclude.

Whilst an exclusion may still be an appropriate sanction, the head teacher should take account of any contributing factors that are identified after an incident of poor behaviour has occurred. For example, where it comes to light that the pupil has suffered bereavement, has mental health issues or has been subject to bullying.

Early intervention to address underlying causes of disruptive behaviour should include an assessment of whether appropriate provision is in place to support any SEN or disability that a pupil may have. The head teacher should also consider the use of a multi-agency assessment for a pupil who demonstrates persistent disruptive behaviour. Such assessments may pick up unidentified SEN but the scope of the assessment could go further, for example, by seeking to identify mental health or family problems[7].

Where a pupil has received multiple exclusions or is approaching the legal limit of 45 school days of fixed-period exclusion in an academic year, the head teacher should consider whether exclusion is providing an effective sanction.

Statutory guidance to the head teacher on the exclusion of pupils from groups with disproportionately high rates of exclusion

The exclusion rates for certain groups of pupils are consistently higher than average. This includes: pupils with SEN; pupils eligible for free school meals; looked after children[8]; and pupils from certain ethnic groups. The ethnic groups with the highest rates of exclusion are: Gypsy/Roma; Travellers of Irish Heritage; and Caribbean pupils.

In addition to the approaches on early intervention set out above, the head teacher should consider what extra support might be needed to identify and address the needs of pupils from these groups in order to reduce their risk of exclusion. For example, schools might draw on the support of Traveller Education Services, or other professionals, to help build trust when engaging with families from Traveller communities.

Statutory guidance to the head teacher on the exclusion of pupils with Education, Health and Care plans (EHC plans)[9] and looked after children

As well as having disproportionately high rates of exclusion, there are certain groups of pupils with additional needs who are particularly vulnerable to the impacts of exclusion. This includes pupils with EHC plans and looked after children. The head teacher should, as far as possible, avoid permanently excluding any pupil with an EHC plan or a looked after child.

Schools should engage proactively with parents in supporting the behaviour of pupils with additional needs. In relation to looked after children, schools should co-operate proactively with foster carers or children's home workers, the local authority that looks after the child and the local authority's virtual school head.

Where a school has concerns about the behaviour, or risk of exclusion, of a child with additional needs, a pupil with an EHC plan or a looked after child, it should, in partnership with others (including the local authority as necessary), consider what additional support or alternative placement may be required. This should involve assessing the suitability of provision for a pupil's SEN. Where a pupil has an EHC plan, schools should consider requesting an early annual review or interim/emergency review.

The head teacher's duty to inform parties about an exclusion

The head teacher's duty to inform parents about an exclusion

A guide to the law[10]

Whenever a head teacher excludes a pupil they must, without delay, notify parents of the period of the exclusion and the reason(s) for it.

They must also, without delay, provide parents with the following information in writing:

the reason(s) for the exclusion;

the period of a fixed-period exclusion or, for a permanent exclusion, the fact that it is permanent;

parents' right to make representations about the exclusion to the governing board (in line with the requirements set out in paragraphs 52 to 60) and how the pupil may be involved in this;

how any representations should be made; and

where there is a legal requirement for the governing board to consider the exclusion, that parents have a right to attend a meeting, to be represented at that meeting (at their own expense) and to bring a friend.

Written notification of the information mentioned in the above paragraph 27 can be provided by delivering it directly to the parents, leaving it at their usual or last known home address, or posting it to that address. Notices can be given electronically if the parents have given written agreement for this kind of notice to be sent in this way[11].

Where an excluded pupil is of compulsory school age the head teacher must also notify the pupil's parents of the days on which they must ensure that the pupil is not present in a public place at any time during school hours. These days would be the first five school days of an exclusion (or until the start date of any alternative provision or the end of the exclusion where this is earlier). Any parent who fails to comply with this duty without reasonable justification commits an offence and may be given a fixed penalty notice or be prosecuted. The head teacher must notify the parents of the days on which their duty applies without delay and, at the latest, by the end of the afternoon session[12].

If alternative provision is being arranged, then the following information must be included with this notice where it can reasonably be found out within the timescale:

the start date for any provision of full-time education that has been arranged for the child during the exclusion;

the start and finish times of any such provision, including the times for morning and afternoon sessions where relevant;

the address at which the provision will take place; and

any information required by the pupil to identify the person they should report to on the first day.

Where this information on alternative provision is not reasonably ascertainable by the end of the afternoon session, it may be provided in a subsequent notice, but it must be provided without delay and no later than 48 hours before the provision is due to start. The only exception to this is where alternative provision is to be provided before the sixth day of an exclusion, in which case the information can be provided with less than 48 hours' notice with parents' consent.

The information in paragraphs 29 to 31 must be provided in writing but can be provided by any effective method (paragraph 37 provides guidance on this issue).

The failure of a head teacher to give notice of the information in paragraphs 29 and 30 by the required time does not relieve the head of the duty to serve the notice. A notice is not made invalid solely because it has not been given by the required time.

If a child is excluded for a further fixed-period following their original exclusion, or is subsequently permanently excluded, the head teacher must inform parents without delay and issue a new exclusion notice to parents.

Statutory guidance to the head teacher on informing parents about an exclusion

For notifications under paragraph 26, although this must not delay notification, ideally, notification should be in person or by telephone in the first instance as this would give the parents an opportunity to ask any initial questions or raise concerns directly with the head teacher.

When notifying parents about an exclusion, the head teacher should set out what arrangements have been made to enable the pupil to continue their education prior to the start of any alternative provision or the pupil's return to school, in line with legal requirements and guidance in section 5.

For notifications under paragraphs 29 and 30, effective methods for providing the information may include email or text message, giving the notice directly to the parents, or sending the information home with the excluded pupil. Where information is sent home with the pupil, the head teacher should consider sending a duplicate copy by an alternative method or confirming that the information has been received

When notifying parents about an exclusion, the head teacher should draw attention to relevant sources of free and impartial information. This information should include:

a link to this statutory guidance on exclusions (https://www.gov.uk/government/publications/school-exclusion);

a link to sources of impartial advice for parents such as the Coram Children's Legal Centre (www.childrenslegalcentre.com), or ACE Education (http://www.ace-ed.org.uk) and their advice line service on 03000 115 142 on Monday to Wednesday from 10 am to 1 pm during term time); and

where considered relevant by the head teacher, links to local services, such as Traveller Education Services, the Information Advice & Support Services Network (formerly known as the local parent partnership) (https://councilfordisabledchildren.org.uk/information-advice-and-support-services-network/about), the National Autistic Society (NAS) School Exclusion Service (England) (0808 800 4002 or schoolexclusions@nas.org.uk), or Independent Parental Special Education Advice (http://www.ipsea.org.uk/).

The head teacher should ensure that information provided to parents is clear and easily understood. Where the parents' first language is not English consideration should be given, where practical, to translating the letter or taking additional steps to ensure that the details of the exclusion and their right to make representations to the governing board have been understood.

The head teacher's duty to inform the governing board and the local authority about an exclusion

A guide to the law[13]

The head teacher must, without delay, notify the governing board and the local authority of:

any permanent exclusion (including where a fixed-period exclusion is followed by a decision to permanently exclude the pupil);

any exclusion which would result in the pupil being excluded for a total of more than five school days (or more than ten lunchtimes) in a term; and

any exclusion which would result in the pupil missing a public examination or national curriculum test.

The head teacher must also notify the local authority and governing board once per term of any other exclusions not already notified.

Notifications must include the reason(s) for the exclusion and the duration of any fixed-period exclusion.

In addition, within 14 days of a request, a governing board must provide to the Secretary of State and (in the case of maintained schools and PRUs) the local authority, information about any exclusions within the last 12 months[14].

For a permanent exclusion, if the pupil lives outside the local authority area in which the school is located, the head teacher must also notify the pupil's 'home authority' of the exclusion and the reason(s) for it without delay.

5. The governing board's and local authority's duties to arrange education for excluded pupils

A guide to the law[15]

For a fixed-period exclusion of more than five school days, the governing board (or local authority in relation to a pupil excluded from a PRU) must arrange suitable full-time education for any pupil of compulsory school age. This provision must begin no later than the sixth school day of the exclusion. Where a child receives consecutive fixed-period exclusions, these are regarded as a cumulative period of exclusion for the purposes of this duty. This means that if a child has more than five consecutive school days of exclusion, then education must be arranged for the sixth school day of exclusion, regardless of whether this is as a result of one fixed-period or more than one fixed-period exclusion.

For permanent exclusions, the local authority must arrange suitable full-time education for the pupil to begin no later than the sixth school day of the exclusion[16]. This will be the pupil's 'home authority' in cases where the school is maintained by (or located within) a different local authority.

In addition, where a pupil has an EHC plan, the local authority may need to review the plan or reassess the child's needs, in consultation with parents, with a view to identifying a new placement[17].

The local authority must have regard to the relevant statutory guidance when carrying out its duties in relation to the education of looked after children.

Provision does not have to be arranged by either the school or the local authority for a pupil in the final year of compulsory education who does not have any further public examinations to sit.

Statutory guidance on the education of pupils prior to the sixth day of an exclusion

It is important for schools to help minimise the disruption that exclusion can cause to an excluded pupil's education. Whilst the statutory duty on governing boards or local authorities is to provide full-time education from the sixth day of an exclusion, there is an obvious benefit in starting this provision as soon as possible. In particular, in the case of a looked after child, the school and the local authority should work together to arrange alternative provision from the first day following the exclusion

Where it is not possible, or not appropriate, to arrange alternative provision during the first five school days of an exclusion, the school should take reasonable steps to set and mark work for the pupil. Work that is provided should be accessible and achievable by the pupil outside school.

The governing board's duty to consider an exclusion

The requirements on a governing board to consider an exclusion

A guide to the law[18]

The governing board has a duty to consider parents' representations about an exclusion. The requirements on a governing board to consider an exclusion depend upon a number of factors (these requirements are illustrated by the diagram in Annex A of this guidance, *A summary of the governing board's duties to review the head teacher's exclusion decision*).

In the case of a maintained school, the governing board may delegate its functions with respect to the consideration of an exclusion to a designated sub-committee consisting of at least three governors.

In the case of an academy, the governing board may delegate to a smaller sub-committee if the trust's articles of association allow them to do so.

The governing board must consider the reinstatement of an excluded pupil within 15 school days[19] of receiving notice of the exclusion if:

the exclusion is permanent;

it is a fixed-period exclusion which would bring the pupil's total number of school days of exclusion to more than 15 in a term; or

it would result in a pupil missing a public examination or national curriculum test.

The requirements are different for fixed-period exclusions where a pupil would be excluded for more than five but less than 15 school days in the term. In this case, if the parents make representations, the governing board must consider within 50 school days of receiving the notice of exclusion whether the excluded pupil should be reinstated. In the absence of any representations from the parents, the governing board is not required to meet and cannot direct the reinstatement of the pupil.

Where an exclusion would result in a pupil missing a public examination or national curriculum test, there is a further requirement for a governing board. It must, so far as is reasonably practicable, consider the exclusion before the date of the examination or test. If it is not practicable for a sufficient number of governors to consider the decision before the examination or test, the chair of governors, in the case of a maintained school may consider the exclusion alone and decide whether or not to reinstate the pupil[20]. In the case of an academy the exclusion may be considered by a smaller sub-committee if the trust's articles of association allow them to do so. In such cases, parents still have the right to make representations to the governing board and must be made aware of this right.

The following parties must be invited to a meeting of the governing board and allowed to make representations:

parents (and, where requested, a representative or friend);

the head teacher; and

a representative of the local authority (in the case of a maintained school or PRU)[21].

The governing board must make reasonable endeavours to arrange the meeting for a date and time that is convenient to all parties, but in compliance with the relevant statutory time limits set out above. However, its decision will not be invalid simply on the grounds that it was not made within these time limits.

In the case of a fixed-period exclusion which does not bring the pupil's total number of days of exclusion to more than five in a term, the governing board must consider any representations made by parents, but it cannot direct reinstatement and is not required to arrange a meeting with parents.

Statutory guidance to a governing board in preparing for the consideration of an exclusion

Where the governing board is legally required to consider the reinstatement of an excluded pupil they should:

not discuss the exclusion with any party outside the meeting;

ask for any written evidence in advance of the meeting (including witness statements and other relevant information held by the school such as those relating to a pupil's SEN);

where possible, circulate any written evidence and information, including a list of those who will be present, to all parties at least five school days in advance of the meeting;

allow parents and the pupil to be accompanied by a friend or representative (where a pupil under 18 is to be invited as a witness, the governing boardshould first seek parental consent and invite the parents to accompany their child to the meeting);

comply with their duty to make reasonable adjustments for people who use the school and consider what reasonable adjustments should be made to support the attendance and contribution of parties at the meeting (for example where a parent or pupil has a disability in relation to mobility or communication that has an impact upon their ability to attend the meeting or to make representations); and

identify the steps they will take to enable and encourage the excluded pupil to attend the meeting and speak on their own behalf (such as providing accessible information or allowing them to bring a friend), taking into account the pupil's age and understanding; or how the excluded pupil may feed in their views by other means if attending the exclusion meeting is not possible.

Statutory guidance to a governing board on exclusions that would result in a pupil missing a public examination or national curriculum test

Whilst there is no automatic right for an excluded pupil to take an examination or test on the excluding school's premises, the governing board should consider whether it would be appropriate to exercise its discretion to allow an excluded pupil onto the premises for the sole purpose of taking the examination or test.

The requirements on a governing board when considering the reinstatement of an excluded pupil

A guide to the law[22]

Where the governing board is legally required to consider reinstating an excluded pupil, they must consider the interests and circumstances of the excluded pupil, including the circumstances in which the pupil was excluded, and have regard to the interests of other pupils and people working at the school.

The governing board must also consider any representations made by or on behalf of:

parents;

the head teacher; and

the local authority (in the case of a maintained school or PRU).

When establishing the facts in relation to an exclusion the governing board must apply the civil standard of proof; i.e. 'on the balance of probabilities' (it is more likely than not that a fact is true) rather than the criminal standard of 'beyond reasonable doubt'.

In the light of its consideration, the governing board can either:

decline to reinstate the pupil; or

direct reinstatement of the pupil immediately or on a particular date.

Where reinstatement would make no practical difference because for example, the pupil has already returned to school following the expiry of a fixed-period exclusion or the parents make clear they do not want their child reinstated, the governing board must still consider whether the pupil should be officially reinstated. If it decides against reinstatement of a pupil who has been permanently excluded the parents can request an independent review.

Statutory guidance to a governing board on considering the reinstatement of an excluded pupil

The governing board should identify the steps they will take to ensure all parties will be supported to participate in its consideration and have their views properly heard. This is particularly important where pupils aged under 18 are speaking about their own exclusion or giving evidence to the governing board.

The governing board should ensure that clear minutes are taken of the meeting as a record of the evidence that was considered by the governing board. These minutes should be made available to all parties on request.

The governing board should ask all parties to withdraw before making a decision. Where present, a clerk may stay to help the governing board by reference to their notes of the meeting and with the wording of the decision letter.

In reaching a decision on whether or not a pupil should be reinstated, the governing board should consider whether the decision to exclude the pupil was lawful, reasonable and procedurally fair, taking account of the head teacher's legal duties and any evidence that was presented to the governing board in relation to the decision to exclude.

The governing board should note the outcome of its consideration on the pupil's educational record, along with copies of relevant papers for future reference.

In cases where the governing board considers parents' representations but does not have the power to direct a pupil's reinstatement, it should consider whether it would be appropriate to place a note of its findings on the pupil's educational record.

Claims of discrimination to the First-tier Tribunal (Special Educational Needs and Disability), in relation to disability, or County Court, for all other forms of discrimination, can be made up to six months after the discrimination is alleged to have occurred. Where practicable, schools should retain records and evidence relating to an exclusion for at least six months in case such a claim is made.

The governing board's duty to notify people after its consideration of reinstatement

A guide to the law[23]

Where legally required to consider reinstating an excluded pupil, the governing board must notify parents, the head teacher and the local authority of its decision, and the reasons for it, in writing and without delay. Where the pupil resides in a different local authority area from the one in which the school is located, the governing board must also inform the pupil's 'home authority'.

In the case of a permanent exclusion where the governing board decides not to reinstate the pupil, the governing board's notification must also include the information below.

The fact that it is permanent.

Notice of parents' right to ask for the decision to be reviewed by an independent review panel and the following information:

the date by which an application for a review must be made (i.e. 15 school days from the date on which notice in writing of the governing board's decision is given to parents – see paragraph 78);

where and to whom an application for a review (and any written evidence) should be submitted;

that any application should set out the grounds on which it is being made and that, where appropriate, this should include a reference to how the pupil's SEN are considered to be relevant to the exclusion;

that, regardless of whether the excluded pupil has recognised SEN, parents have a right to require the local authority/academy trust to appoint an SEN expert to advise the review panel;

details of the role of the SEN expert; and

that parents may, at their own expense, appoint someone to make written and/or oral representations to the panel.

That, in addition to the right to apply for an independent review panel, if parents believe that there has been unlawful discrimination in relation to the exclusion then they may make a claim under the Equality Act 2010 to the First-tier Tribunal (Special Educational Needs and Disability) in the case of disability discrimination, or the County Court, in the case of other forms of discrimination.

That a claim of discrimination under the Equality Act 2010 made under these routes should be lodged within six months of the date on which the discrimination is alleged to have taken place (e.g. the day on which the pupil was excluded).

The governing board may provide the information in paragraphs 75 and 76 by delivering it directly to parents, delivering it to their last known address, or posting it first class to that address.

Notice is deemed to have been given on the same day if it is delivered or on the second working day after posting if it is sent by first class mail.

Statutory guidance to a governing board on providing information to parents following its consideration of an exclusion

The governing board should set out the reasons for its decision in sufficient detail to enable all parties to understand why the decision was made.

Where relevant, it will be for the governing board to confirm the details of where the parents' application for an independent review panel should be sent. This is normally the clerk of the independent review panel. The notice should make it clear that parents are entitled to bring a friend to the review.

In providing details of the role of the SEN expert, the governing board should refer to the statutory guidance provided to SEN experts in paragraphs 164 to 167. The notice should explain that there would be no cost to parents for this appointment and that parents must make clear if they wish for an SEN expert to be appointed in any application for a review.

Where the governing board declines to reinstate the pupil, it should draw the attention of parents to relevant sources of free and impartial information that will allow them to make an informed decision on whether and, if so, how to seek a review of the decision. This information should be included in the letter notifying parents of a decision to uphold an exclusion, which should also include:

a link to this statutory guidance on exclusions (https://www.gov.uk/government/publications/school-exclusion);

a link to guidance on making a claim of discrimination to the First-tier Tribunal (Special Educational Needs and Disability) (https://www.gov.uk/courts- tribunals/first-tier-tribunal-special-educational-needs-and-disability) or the County Court;

a link to sources of impartial advice for parents such as the Coram Children's Legal Centre (www.childrenslegalcentre.com) or ACE Education (http://www.ace- ed.org.uk) and their limited advice line service on 03000 115 142 on Monday to Wednesday from 10 am to 1 pm during term time); and

where considered relevant by the head teacher, links to local services, such as Traveller Education Services, the Information Advice & Support Services Network (formerly known as the local parent partnership) (https://councilfordisabledchildren.org.uk/information-advice-and-support-services- network/about), the National Autistic Society (NAS) School Exclusion Service (England) (0808 800 4002 or schoolexclusions@nas.org.uk), or Independent Parental Special Education Advice (http://www.ipsea.org.uk/).

7. The governing board's duty to remove a permanently excluded pupil's name from the school register

A guide to the law[24]

The governing board must ensure that a pupil's name is removed from the school admissions register if:

15 school days have passed since the parents were notified of the governing board's decision to not reinstate the pupil and no application has been made for an independent review panel; or

the parents have stated in writing that they will not be applying for an independent review panel.

Where an application for an independent review panel has been made within 15 school days, the school must wait until the review has been determined, or abandoned, and until the governing board has completed any reconsideration that the panel has recommended or directed it to carry out, before removing a pupil's name from the register. Where a pupil's name is to be deleted from the school admissions register because of a permanent exclusion the school must make a return to the local authority. The return must include all the particulars which were entered in the admission register, the address of any parent with whom the pupil normally resides and the grounds upon which their name is to be deleted from the admissions register (i.e. permanent exclusion). This return must be made as soon as the grounds for deletion is met and no later than the deletion of the pupil's name.

Where a pupil's name is removed from the school register and a discrimination claim is subsequently made, the First-tier Tribunal (Special Educational Needs and Disability) or County Court has the power to direct that the pupil should be reinstated.

Guidance to schools on marking attendance registers following exclusion

Whilst an excluded pupil's name remains on a school's admissions register, the pupil should be marked using the appropriate attendance code. Where alternative provision has been made and the pupil attends it, an appropriate attendance code, such as Code D (if the alternative provision is at a PRU or independent school where the pupil is dual registered) or Code B (if the provision is an approved educational activity that does not involve the pupil being registered at any other school), should be used. Where pupils are not attending alternative provision, they should be marked absent using Code E[25].

Arranging a date and venue

A guide to the law[26]

If applied for by parents within the legal time frame, the local authority or (in the case of an academy) the academy trust must, at their own expense, arrange for an independent review panel hearing to review the decision of a governing board not to reinstate a permanently excluded pupil.

The legal time frame for an application is:

within 15 school days of notice being given to the parents by the governing board of its decision not to reinstate a permanently excluded pupil (in accordance with the requirements summarised in paragraph 75); or

where an application has not been made within this time frame, within 15 school days of the final determination of a claim of discrimination under the Equality Act 2010 in relation to the exclusion[27].

Any application made outside of the legal time frame must be rejected by the local authority/academy trust.

The local authority/academy trust must not delay or postpone arranging an independent review panel where parents also make a claim of discrimination in relation to the exclusion to the First-tier Tribunal (Special Educational Needs and Disability) or the County Court[28].

Parents may request an independent review panel even if they did not make representations to, or attend, the meeting at which the governing board considered reinstating the pupil.

The local authority/academy trust must take reasonable steps to identify a date for the review that all parties, and any SEN expert appointed to give advice in person, are able to attend. However, the review must begin within 15 school days of the day on which the parent's application for a review was made (panels have the power to adjourn a hearing if required).

The venue must be accessible to all parties[29].

The local authority/academy trust must arrange a venue for hearing the review. Whatever the venue, the panel must hold the hearing in private unless the local authority/academy trust directs otherwise.

Where the issues raised by two or more applications for review are the same, or connected, the panel may combine the reviews if, after consultation with all parties, there are no objections.

Statutory guidance to the local authority and academy trust on arranging a date and venue for a review

The local authority/academy trust should take all reasonable steps to ensure the venue for the review is appropriate and has a suitable area for the parties to wait separately from the panel before the review.

Where the issues raised by two or more applications for review are the same, or connected, but the panel does not combine the reviews the local authority / academy trust should take reasonable steps to ensure fairness and consistency. Where possible, the same panel members should hear all related reviews.

Appointing panel members

A guide to the law[30]

The local authority/academy trust must constitute the panel with either three or five members (as decided by the local authority/academy trust) representing each of the three categories below. A five member panel must be constituted with two members from each of the categories of school governors and head teachers[31].

A lay member to chair the panel who has not worked in any school in a paid capacity, disregarding any experience as a school governor or volunteer.

Current or former school governors (including members of PRU management committees and directors of academy trusts) who have served as a governor for at least 12 consecutive months in the last five years, provided they have not been teachers or head teachers during that time.

Head teachers or individuals who have been a head teacher within the last five years.

A person may not serve as a member of a review panel if they:

are a member/director of the local authority/academy trust or governing board of the excluding school;

are the head teacher of the excluding school or anyone who has held this position in the last five years;

are an employee of the local authority/academy trust, or the governing board, of the excluding school (unless they are employed as a head teacher at another school);

have, or at any time have had, any connection with the local authority/academy trust, school, governing board, parents or pupil, or the incident leading to the exclusion, which might reasonably be taken to raise doubts about their impartiality (though an individual must not be taken to have such a connection simply because they are employed by the local authority/academy trust as a head teacher at another school); or

have not had the required training within the last two years (see paragraph 124).

In relation to panel members appointed by the local authority, sections 173(4) and 174(1) of the Local Government Act 1972 apply when determining allowances for financial loss, travel or subsistence. It is for the academy trust to determine its own payment arrangements for panel members.

The local authority/academy trust must make arrangements to indemnify panel members against any legal costs and expenses reasonably incurred as a result of any decisions or actions connected to the review which are taken in good faith.

Statutory guidance to the local authority/academy trust on appointing independent review panel members

Every care should be taken to avoid bias or an appearance of bias. The local authority/academy trust should request that prospective panel members declare any conflict of interest at the earliest opportunity.

Where possible, panel members who are governors or head teachers should reflect the phase of education (primary/secondary) and type of school from which the pupil was excluded, for example: special school; boarding school; PRU; academy or maintained school.

The local authority/academy trust should consider whether the chair should be someone with a legal qualification or other legal experience. This is particularly important where a clerk will not be providing legal expertise to the panel.

In order to meet their duties within the statutory time frame, the local authority/academy trust should identify a number of eligible individuals in each of the different categories required to constitute an independent review panel in advance of an application for a review.

Appointing a clerk and the clerk's role

A guide to the law [32]

The local authority/academy trust may appoint a clerk to provide advice to the panel and parties to the review on procedure, law and statutory guidance onexclusions.

Where appointed the clerk must perform the following additional functions:

Make reasonable efforts to inform the following people that they are entitled to: make written representations to the panel; attend the hearing and make oral representations to the panel; and be represented:

the parents;

the head teacher;

the governing board; and

the local authority (in the case of a maintained school or PRU).

Make reasonable efforts to circulate to all parties copies of relevant papers at least 5 school days before the review. These papers must include:

the governing board's decision;

the parents' application for a review; and

any policies or documents that the governing board was required to have regard to in making its decision.

Give all parties details of those attending and their role, once the position is clear.

Attend the review and ensure that minutes are produced in accordance with instructions from the panel.

Where a clerk is not appointed, the functions in paragraph 107 become the responsibility of the local authority/academy trust.

Statutory guidance to the local authority/academy trust on appointing an independent review panel clerk

The clerk should not have served as clerk to the governing board in the meeting at which the decision was made not to reinstate the pupil.

In addition to the training required by law, clerks should have an up to date understanding of developments in case law which are relevant to exclusion.

Where a clerk is not appointed, the local authority/academy trust should consider what additional steps it may need to take to ensure that the independent review panel is administered properly.

Statutory guidance to local authority/academy trust regarding the clerk's role on preparing for an independent review

The local authority/academy trust should ensure the clerk follows the advice below (paragraphs 113 to 123).

The clerk should identify in advance of the meeting whether the pupil will be attending. Where an excluded pupil is attending the hearing, consideration should be given in advance as to the steps that will be taken to support his/her participation. If the excluded pupil is not attending, it should be made clear that they may feed in their views through a representative or by submitting a written statement.

The clerk should inform the parents of their right to bring a friend to the hearing.

In order to review the governing board's decision, the panel will generally need to hear from those involved in the incident, or incidents, leading to the exclusion. The clerk should also try to ascertain whether an alleged victim, if there is one, wishes to be given a voice at the review. This could be in person, through a representative or by submitting a written statement.

In the case of witnesses who are pupils of the school it will normally be more appropriate for the panel to rely on written statements. Pupils may appear as witnesses if they do so voluntarily and, if they are under 18, with their parents' consent. In such cases, that pupil's parents should be invited to attend the meeting in support of their child.

Where character witnesses are proposed, the clerk should seek the agreement of the panel; but this should be allowed unless there is good reason to refuse.

All written witness statements should be attributed, signed and dated, unless the school has good reason to wish to protect the anonymity of the witness, in which case the statement should at least be dated and labelled in a way that allows it to be distinguished from other statements. The general principle remains that excluded pupils are entitled to know the substance behind the reason for their exclusion.

Parties attending the hearing have the right to be represented. Representatives may make written or oral representations to the panel. If any of the parties wish to bring more than one friend or representative, the clerk should seek the panel's agreement in advance, having regard to a reasonable limit on numbers attending the review. However, all parents may attend, if they wish to do so, and each can make representations and be represented.

In addition to written witness statements, the clerk should request written evidence from the school in order to circulate it in advance of the meeting, such as policies and documents of the school which the governing board would reasonably have been expected to take account of in reaching its decision on reinstatement.

Where the school's case rests largely or solely on physical evidence, and where the facts are in dispute, then the physical evidence, if practicable, should be retained and be available to the panel. Where there are difficulties in retaining physical evidence, photographs or signed witness statements should be used.

Where an excluding head teacher has left the school, the panel may use its discretion in deciding whether to also invite this person to make representations.

The clerk should notify the panel where requested documents have not been provided so that the panel can take a decision on whether to adjourn the hearing to allow for the documents to be provided.

Ensuring that panel members and clerks are trained

A guide to the law[33]

124. The local authority/academy trust must ensure that all panel members and clerks have received training within the two years prior to the date of the review. This training must have covered:

the requirements of the primary legislation, regulations and statutory guidance governing exclusions (which would include an understanding of how the principles applicable in an application for judicial review relate to the panel's decision- making);

the need for the panel to observe procedural fairness and the rules of natural justice;

the role of the chair of a review panel;

the role of the clerk to a review panel;

the duties of head teachers, governing boards and the panel under the Equality Act 2010; and

the effect of section 6 of the Human Rights Act 1998 (acts of public authorities unlawful if not compatible with certain human rights) and the need to act in a manner compatible with human rights protected by that Act.

Appointing an SEN expert

A guide to the law[34]

If requested by parents with their application for an independent review panel, the local authority/academy trust must appoint a SEN expert to attend the panel and must cover the associated costs of this appointment.

The SEN expert must be someone who has expertise and experience of special educational needs considered by the local authority/academy trust as appropriate to perform the functions specified in the legislation.

The local authority/academy trust must make arrangements to indemnify the SEN expert against any legal costs and expenses reasonably incurred as a result of any decisions or actions connected to the review and which are taken in good faith.

Parents have a right to request the attendance of an SEN expert at a review, regardless of whether the school recognises that their child has SEN.

The SEN expert's role is set out in paragraphs 164 to 167.

Individuals may not serve as an SEN expert if they have, or at any time have had, any connection with the local authority, academy trust, school, parents or pupil, or the incident leading to the exclusion, which might reasonably be taken to raise doubts about their ability to act impartially. However, an individual should not be assumed to have such a connection simply by virtue of the fact that he/she is an employee of the local authority/academy trust.

Statutory guidance to the local authority and the academy trust on appointing an SEN expert

The SEN expert should be a professional with first-hand experience of the assessment and support of SEN, as well as an understanding of the legal requirements on schools in relation to SEN and disability. Examples of suitable individuals might include educational psychologists; specialist SEN teachers; special educational needs coordinators (SENCOs); and behaviour support teachers. Recently retired individuals are not precluded from fulfilling this role, though the local authority/academy trust would need to assure themselves that the individual had a good understanding of current practice and the legal requirements on schools in relation to SEN.

Whilst individuals are not automatically taken to be partial simply because they are an employee of, or contracted by, a local authority or academy trust, they should not have had any previous involvement in the assessment or support of SEN for the excluded pupil, or siblings of the excluded pupil. The local authority/academy trust should request that prospective SEN experts declare any conflict of interest at the earliest opportunity.

The final decision on the appointment of an SEN expert is for the local authority/academy trust to make but it should take reasonable steps to ensure that parents have confidence in the impartiality and capability of the SEN expert. Where possible, this may include offering parents a choice of SEN expert. In order to meet its duties within the statutory time frame, the local authority/academy trust should consider maintaining a list of individuals capable of performing the role of SEN expert in advance of a request.

It is for the local authority/academy trust to determine the amount of any payment in relation to the appointment of the SEN expert, such as financial loss, travel and subsistence allowances.

9. The duties of independent review panel members, the clerk and the SEN expert in the conduct of an independent review panel

A guide to the law[35]

Panel members and, if appointed, the SEN expert must declare any known conflict of interest to the local authority/academy trust before the start of the review.

The role of the panel is to review the governing board's decision not to reinstate a permanently excluded pupil. In reviewing the decision the panel must consider the interests and circumstances of the excluded pupil, including the circumstances in which the pupil was excluded, and have regard to the interests of other pupils and people working at the school.

The panel must apply the civil standard of proof; i.e. 'on the balance of probabilities' it is more likely than not that a fact is true, rather than the criminal standard of 'beyond reasonable doubt'. This means that the panel should accept that something happened if it is more likely that it happened than that it did not happen.

Following its review, the panel can decide to:

uphold the governing board's decision;

recommend that the governing board reconsiders reinstatement; or

quash the decision and direct that the governing board reconsiders reinstatement.

The panel's decision does not have to be unanimous and can be decided by a majority vote. In the case of a tied vote, the chair has the casting vote.

The independent review panel's decision is binding on the: pupil; parents; governing board; head teacher; and local authority.

The panel may only quash a governing board's decision if it considers that it was flawed when considered in the light of the principles applicable on an application for judicial review (statutory guidance on this consideration is provided by paragraphs 157 to 162).

New evidence may be presented to the panel, though the school may not introduce new reasons for the exclusion or for the decision not to reinstate the pupil and the panel must disregard any new reasons that are introduced.

In deciding whether the governing board's decision was flawed, and therefore whether to quash the decision, the panel must only take account of the evidence that was available to the governing board at the time of it making its decision not to reinstate. This includes any evidence that the panel considers would, or should, have been available to the governing board and that it ought to have taken into account if it had been acting reasonably.

If evidence is presented that the panel considers it is unreasonable to have expected the governing board to have been aware of at the time of its decision, the panel can take account of the evidence when deciding whether to recommend that the governing board reconsider reinstatement.

Where present, the panel must seek and have regard to the SEN expert's view of how SEN might be relevant to the pupil's exclusion. Where a SEN expert has been requested but is not present, the panel should make parents aware of their right to request that the review is adjourned until such time as an SEN expert can attend.

The jurisdiction of the First-tier Tribunal (Special Educational Needs and Disability) and County Court to hear claims of discrimination relating to a permanent exclusion does not preclude an independent review panel from considering issues of discrimination in reaching its decision.

If a panel directs a governing board to reconsider reinstatement it may order the local authority to make an adjustment to the school's budget or (in the case of an academy) the academy trust to make an equivalent payment to the local authority in whose area the school is located, unless within ten school days of receiving notice of the panel's decision, the governing board decides to reinstate the pupil. Paragraph 163 provides statutory guidance to panels on the circumstances under which this payment should not be ordered. The sum of this adjustment/payment must be £4,000 and would be in addition to any funding that would normally follow an excluded pupil. The panel does not have the power to order a financial readjustment or payment in circumstances where it has only recommended that the governing board reconsiders reinstatement of the pupil.

The panel may adjourn on more than one occasion, if necessary. However, consideration must be given to the effect of adjournment on the parties to the review, the excluded pupil and their parents, and any victim.

A review cannot continue if the panel no longer has representation from each of the three categories of members required (see paragraph 98). In this event, the panel may be adjourned until the number can be restored.

Once a review has begun, no panel member may be substituted by a new member for any reason. Accordingly, if the required representation cannot be restored from the original members, a new panel must be constituted to conduct the review afresh. In the case of a five-member panel, the panel may continue in the absence of any of its members, provided all three categories of member are still represented.

Following the review, the panel must issue written notification to all parties without delay. This notification must include:

the panel's decision and the reasons for it;

where relevant, details of any financial readjustment/payment to be made if a governing board subsequently decides not to offer to reinstate a pupil; and

any information that the panel has directed the governing board to place on the pupil's educational record.

Statutory guidance to independent review panel members on the conduct of an independent review panel

The chair should outline the procedure to be followed and explain to all parties that the panel is independent of the school, the local authority and (in the case of an academy) the academy trust. The panel should support all parties to participate in the review and ensure that their views are properly heard. The independent review should be conducted in an accessible, unthreatening and non-adversarial manner.

It is for the panel to decide whether any witnesses should stay after giving evidence for the rest of the review, but they should not be present before giving evidence.

In the interests of fairness and transparency, care should be taken to ensure that no one, other than the clerk, is present with the panel in the absence of the other parties. This includes the SEN expert. The panel should ask everyone, apart from the clerk, to withdraw before the panel makes a decision. The clerk may stay to help the panel by referring to the notes of the meeting and providing advice on the wording of the decision letter.

In any event, the panel must always make one of three fundamental decisions: it must uphold the governing board's decision; or recommend reconsideration; or quash the decision. Where parents are not seeking reinstatement for their child, this fact should be acknowledged by the panel, but it should not affect the conduct of the panel or its decision. Recording of the panel's findings on a child's educational record and an acknowledgement by the governing board that it would be appropriate for it to offer to reinstate the pupil are both potential outcomes in these circumstances.

In the event that a panel cannot continue because it no longer has representation from each of the three categories of members required (see paragraph 98) it should, having regard to the particular circumstances and the effect on the parties, victim, and pupil/parent, adjourn to allow reasonable time for enough missing members to become available

Statutory guidance to independent review panel members on coming to a decision

The panel's decision should not be influenced by any stated intention of the parents or pupil not to return to the school. The focus of the panel's decision is whether there are sufficient grounds for them to direct or recommend that the governing board reconsider its decision to uphold the exclusion.

Public law principles underpin good decision-making. All decisions of a governing board must be made in accordance with public law. Panels are expected to understand the legislation that is relevant to exclusions and the legal principles that apply. Head teacher and governing board members of panels are likely to have first-hand experience of the education context that may be relevant to considerations about whether or not a decision was reasonable in the circumstances.

When considering the governing board's decision in light of the principles applicable in an application for judicial review, the panel should apply the followingtests:

Illegality – did the governing board act outside the scope of its legal powers in deciding that the pupil should not be reinstated?

Irrationality – did the governing board rely on irrelevant points, fail to take account of all relevant points, or make a decision so unreasonable that no governing board acting reasonably in such circumstances could have made it?

Procedural impropriety – was the governing board's consideration so procedurally unfair or flawed that justice was clearly not done?

Procedural impropriety means not simply a breach of minor points of procedure but something more substantive, that has a significant impact on the quality of the decision-making process. This will be a judgement for the panel to make, but the following are examples of the types of things that could give rise to procedural impropriety: bias; failing to notify parents of their right to make representations; the governing board making a decision without having given parents an opportunity to make representations; failing to give reasons for a decision; or being a judge in your own cause (for example, if the head teacher who took the decision to exclude were also to vote on whether the pupil should be reinstated).

Where the criteria for quashing a decision have not been met, the panel should consider whether it would be appropriate to recommend that a governing board reconsiders its decision not to reinstate the pupil. This should not be the default option but should be used where evidence or procedural flaws have been identified that do not meet the criteria for quashing the decision, but which the panel believe justify a reconsideration of the governing board's decision. This could include when new evidence presented at the review hearing was not available to the governing board at the time of its decision.

In all other cases the panel should uphold the governing board's decision.

Statutory guidance to independent review panel members on the financial readjustment/payment

In the case of a maintained school or PRU, where a panel has quashed the governing board's decision and directed that it reconsiders, the panel should order that a readjustment must be made to the school's budget, unless within ten school days of receiving notice of the panel's decision, the governing board decides to reinstate the pupil. In the case of an academy, where the panel has quashed the governing board's decision, the panel should order that the academy trust must make a payment directly to the local authority in whose area the academy is located, unless within ten school days of receiving notice of the panel's decision, the governing board decides to reinstate the pupil.

Statutory guidance to SEN experts on their conduct during an independent review panel

The SEN expert's role is analogous to an expert witness, providing impartial specialist advice to the panel on how SEN might be relevant to the exclusion. The SEN expert should base their advice on the evidence provided to the panel. The SEN expert's role does not include making an assessment of the pupil's special educational needs.

The focus of the SEN expert's advice should be on whether the school's policies which relate to SEN, or the application of these policies in relation to the excluded pupil, were lawful, reasonable and procedurally fair (in line with the guidance to panels in paragraph 159). If the SEN expert believes that this was not the case, they should, where possible, advise the panel on the possible contribution that this could have made to the circumstances of the pupil's exclusion.

Where the school does not recognise a pupil as having SEN, the SEN expert should advise the panel on whether they believe the school acted in a legal, reasonable and procedurally fair way with respect to the identification of any SEN that the pupil may potentially have, and any contribution that this could have made to the circumstances of the pupil's exclusion.

The SEN expert should not criticise a school's policies or actions simply because they believe a different approach should have been followed or because another school might have taken a different approach.

Statutory guidance to the clerk and local authority/academy trust on the record of the proceedings of a review panel

The clerk to a review panel should ensure that minutes of the proceedings are taken, including details of the attendance, the voting and the decision.

The minutes are not public documents but should be retained by the local authority/academy trust for a period of at least five years, as they may need to be seen by a court or (in the case of maintained school) by the Public Service Ombudsman. The local authority/academy trust should be aware of its duties under the Freedom of Information Act 2000 and the Data Protection Act 1998 when retaining information.

Statutory guidance to the independent review panel and clerk on notifying parties of the outcome of the review

If the panel upholds the governing board's decision, the clerk should immediately report this to the local authority as well as notifying the parents and governing board. If the pupil lives outside the local authority in which the school is located, the clerk should make sure that the 'home authority' is also informed in writing without delay of the outcome of the review. This includes any situation where parents withdraw or abandon their application for a review.

10. The governing board's duty to reconsider reinstatement following a review

A guide to the law[36]

Where the panel directs or recommends that the governing board reconsider whether a pupil should be reinstated, the governing board must reconvene to do so within ten school days of being given notice of the panel's decision. Notice is deemed to have been given on the day of delivery if it is delivered directly or on the second working day after posting if it is sent by first class mail.

It is important that the governing board conscientiously reconsiders whether the pupil should be reinstated, whether the panel has directed or merely recommended it to do so. Whilst the governing board may still reach the same conclusion as it first did, it may face challenge in the courts if it refuses to reinstate the pupil, without strong justification.

Following a direction to reconsider, unless within ten school days of receiving notice of the panel's decision, the governing board decides to reinstate the pupil an adjustment may be made to the school's budget in the sum of £4,000 if the panel has ordered this. In the case of an academy, the school would be required to make an equivalent payment directly to the local authority in which the school is located. This payment will be in addition to any funding that would normally follow an excludedpupil.

If the governing board offers to reinstate the pupil within the specified timescale but this is declined by the parents, no budget adjustment or payment can be made. The governing board must comply with any direction of the panel to place a note on the pupil's educational record. The clerk must also note, where a pupil is not reinstated following a direction to reconsider, the exclusion does not count towards the rule that an admission authority may refuse to admit a child who has been excluded twice; or in the case of a community or voluntary controlled school, the governing board may appeal against the decision of the local authority as the admission authority to admit thechild.

In the case of either a recommended or directed reconsideration, the governing board must notify the following people of their reconsidered decision, and the reasons for it, in writing and without delay:

the parents;

the head teacher;

the local authority; and, where relevant, the 'home authority'.

Statutory guidance on the governing board's duty to reconsider reinstatement following a review

The reconsideration provides an opportunity for the governing board to look afresh at the question of reinstating the pupil, in light of the findings of the independent review panel. There is no requirement to seek further representations from other parties or to invite them to the reconsideration meeting. The governing board is not prevented from taking into account other matters that it considers relevant. It should, however, take care to ensure that any additional information does not make the decision unlawful. This could be the case, for example, where new evidence is presented, or information is considered that is irrelevant to the decision at hand.

The governing board should ensure that clear minutes are taken of the meeting as a record of the evidence that was considered by the governing board. These minutes should be made available to all parties on request.

The governing board should ask any parties in attendance to withdraw before making a decision. Where present, a clerk may stay to help the governing board by reference to their notes of the meeting and with the wording of the decision letter.

The governing board should note the outcome of its consideration on the pupil's educational record, along with copies of any papers for future reference.

The governing board should base its reconsideration on the presumption that a pupil will return to the school if reinstated, regardless of any stated intentions by the parents or pupil. Any decision of a governing board to offer reinstatement which is subsequently turned down by the parents should be recorded on the pupil's educational record. The governing board's decision should demonstrate how they have addressed the concerns raised by the independent review panel; this should be communicated in standard English for all parties to understand.

11. The local authority's role in overseeing the financial readjustment/payment[37]

A guide to the law

The local authority cannot require a maintained school or academy to make any additional payments following a permanent exclusion, other than the budget share deductions set out in regulations, or the payments which an academy has to make under its funding agreement[38].

The local authority will be responsible for adjusting the budget share for maintained schools and PRUs with delegated budgets if a pupil is permanently excluded, so funding follows the pupil. The process and requirements are set out in the School and Early Years Finance (England) Regulations, issued on an annual basis.

A local authority may ask an academy trust to enter into an arrangement for the transfer of funding for a pupil who has been permanently excluded, on the same basis as if the academy were a maintained school. The academy trust may be obliged under its funding agreement to comply with such a request.

If a review panel has ordered a financial adjustment, the local authority will be responsible for reducing the budget share for the excluding school by a further £4,000. If the excluding school is an academy, the academy trust must pay £4,000 to the local authority.

If a review panel has made a financial adjustment order and the excluded pupil is given a place at another school, including a PRU, ('the admitting school'), the local authority may, if it chooses, pass any or all of the amount of the financial adjustment (i.e. up to £4,000) to the admitting school.

The local authority will be responsible for adjusting the budget share for maintained schools and PRUs with delegated budgets in circumstances where a panel has ordered a financial adjustment (see paragraph 163).

Statutory guidance to the local authority on overseeing the transfer of funding following a permanent exclusion

This financial readjustment should be made within 28 days of notification of a direction from the panel. The academy trust should be expected to make payment to the local authority in which the academy is located within the same timescale.

If an academy fails to comply with its legal requirement to pay following a direction from an independent review panel then the local authority will be responsible for enforcing this requirement. However, the local authority should also inform the Education and Skills Funding Agency.

If an excluded pupil has been found a place at another school by the time the governing board has reconsidered and decided not to reinstate the pupil, the local authority may, if it chooses, pass the amount of the financial readjustment to the pupil's new school.

12. Statutory guidance to the head teacher, governing board and independent review panel members on police involvement and parallel criminal proceedings

The head teacher need not postpone taking a decision on an exclusion solely because a police investigation is underway and/or any criminal proceedings may be brought. In such circumstances, the head teacher will need to take a decision on the evidence available to them at the time.

Where the evidence is limited by a police investigation or criminal proceedings, the head teacher should consider any additional steps they may need to take to ensure that the decision to exclude is fair. However, the final decision on whether to exclude is for the head teacher to make.

Where the governing board is required to consider a reinstatement in these circumstances, it cannot postpone its meeting and must decide whether or not to reinstate the pupil on the evidence available.

The fact that parallel criminal proceedings are in progress should also not directly determine whether an independent review panel should be adjourned. Relevant factors for the panel to consider will include:

whether any charge has been brought against the pupil and, if so, what the charge is;

whether relevant witnesses and documents are available;

the likely length of delay if the hearing were adjourned and the effect it may have on the excluded pupil, the parents, any victim or the school; and

whether an adjournment or declining to adjourn might result in injustice.

Where a panel decides to adjourn, the clerk (or local authority/academy trust where a clerk is not appointed) should monitor the progress of any police investigation and/or criminal proceedings and reconvene the panel at the earliest opportunity. If necessary, the panel may adjourn more than once (in line with the requirements summarised in paragraph 148).

Useful links

Departmental Advice on Alternative Provision:

https://www.gov.uk/government/publications/education-for-children-with-health-needs- who-cannot-attend-school

https://www.gov.uk/government/uploads/system/uploads/attachment_data/file/268940/alternative_provision_statutory_guidance_pdf_version.pdf

Departmental Advice on Behaviour and Discipline in Schools:

https://www.gov.uk/government/publications/behaviour-and-discipline-in-schools

Departmental Advice on Behaviour and Mental Health:

https://www.gov.uk/government/publications/mental-health-and-behaviour-in-schools--2

Children with Special Educational Needs and Disabilities:

https://www.gov.uk/children-with-special-educational-needs/overview

Departmental Advice on attendance:

https://www.gov.uk/government/publications/school-attendance

Annex A – A summary of the governing board's duties to review the head teacher's exclusion decision

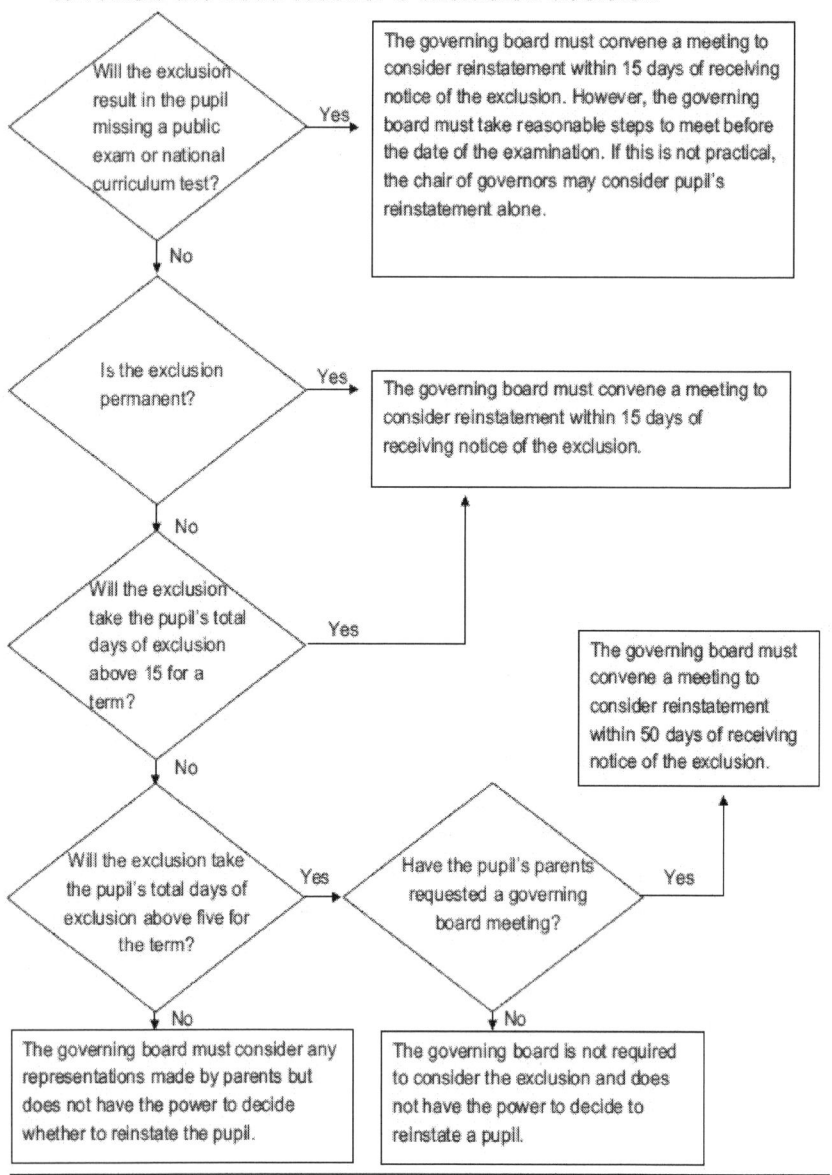

Will the exclusion result in the pupil missing a public exam or national curriculum test?
— Yes → The governing board must convene a meeting to consider reinstatement within 15 days of receiving notice of the exclusion. However, the governing board must take reasonable steps to meet before the date of the examination. If this is not practical, the chair of governors may consider pupil's reinstatement alone.
— No ↓

Is the exclusion permanent?
— Yes → The governing board must convene a meeting to consider reinstatement within 15 days of receiving notice of the exclusion.
— No ↓

Will the exclusion take the pupil's total days of exclusion above 15 for a term?
— Yes → The governing board must convene a meeting to consider reinstatement within 50 days of receiving notice of the exclusion.
— No ↓

Will the exclusion take the pupil's total days of exclusion above five for the term?
— Yes → **Have the pupil's parents requested a governing board meeting?**
  — Yes → The governing board must convene a meeting to consider reinstatement within 50 days of receiving notice of the exclusion.
  — No → The governing board is not required to consider the exclusion and does not have the power to decide to reinstate a pupil.
— No → The governing board must consider any representations made by parents but does not have the power to decide whether to reinstate the pupil.

The governing board may delegate its functions to consider an exclusion to a designated committee. References to days mean 'school days'.

Annex B – A non-statutory guide for head teachers

Exclusion process for head teachers, academy principals and teachers in charge of pupil referral units

This non-statutory document should be read alongside the statutory guidance. This document is meant to help schools through the process and ensure that they have sufficient procedures in place.

Glossary

The term **'must'** refers to what head teachers/governing boards/academy trusts/local authorities and parents are required to do by law. The term **'should'** refers to recommendations for good practice as mentioned in the exclusions guidance.

In this document and in the exclusion guidance, **'parents'** refers to parent(s)/legal guardian(s)/foster carer(s) of pupils under 18, as well as to pupils over 18, and the term **'governing board'** includes the governing body of a maintained school, management committee of a PRU and the academy trust of an academy.

Early Intervention

You[39] must establish a behaviour policy and should have processes for identifying and supporting pupils' additional needs.

Things to consider

Does the school behaviour policy clearly set out behaviour expectations and sanctions and reflect the requirements of the Equality Act 2010?

Are governors/staff (including sixth form staff in school sixth forms) clear about their roles and when to escalate issues/involve parents?

Is the behaviour policy understood by pupils and parents?

Are sanctions monitored to identify any inconsistency or potential discrimination (e.g. Special Educational Needs and Disability (SEND) or ethnicity)?

Are systems in place to identify pupils showing persistent poor behaviour and if there are any underlying causes?

Further sources of information

Departmental advice on setting the behaviour policy https://www.gov.uk/government/publications/behaviour-and-discipline-in-schools

What maintained schools must publish online https://www.gov.uk/guidance/what- maintained-schools-must-publish-online

What academies, free schools and colleges must publish online https://www.gov.uk/guidance/what-academies-free-schools-and-colleges-should-publish- online

You should have a system in place to ensure you are aware of any pupil showing persistent poor behaviour or not responding to low level sanctions.

Things to consider

Are underlying factors (for example SEND, family issues or bullying) or specific triggers (for example the time of day or specific lessons) affecting behaviour? Are staff working with the pupil aware of any behavioural trigger points, relevant issues and the ways in which they should be managed?

Are staff aware of mechanisms for escalation and referral routes to access external support?

Have I ensured that this pupil's parents are aware of their behaviour issues?

Should I request an special educational needs (SEN) assessment, a multi-agency assessment or external support (e.g. counsellors or alternative provision)?

Did I consider if the pupil was a looked after child? (e.g. did I engage with foster carers or children's home workers, the local authority that looks after the child and the local authority's virtual school head?)

Is the use and effectiveness of any support and sanctions properly recorded and regularly reviewed?

Further sources of information

Guidance on the use of alternative provision https://www.gov.uk/government/publications/alternative-provision

You should have a clear process in place for exclusion.

Things to consider

Are there clear processes and templates in place to:

monitor the 45-day exclusion rule, including exclusions received from other schools?

manage serious behavioural incidents when I am not available?

avoid wherever possible the permanent exclusion of those with Education, Health and Care plans or Statements of SEN and looked after children.

inform the parents, governing board and local authority (depending on length of exclusion), clearly setting out all reasons for the exclusion?

give up-to-date links to sources of impartial advice for parents?

reintegrate excluded pupils after a fixed period exclusion and support pupils' future behaviour?

arrange, at short notice, suitable full-time alternative education for pupils receiving exclusions over five days?

Further sources of information

Information on school discipline and exclusions issued by the Department for Education https://www.gov.uk/school-discipline-exclusions/exclusions

Coram Children's Legal Centre http://www.childrenslegalcentre.com/index.php?page=school_exclusions

ACE Education also run a limited advice line service on 03000 115 142 on Monday to Wednesday from 10 am to 1 pm during term time. Information can be found on their website: http://www.ace-ed.org.uk/

National Autistic Society (NAS) School Exclusion Service (England) can be contacted on 0808 800 4002 or via schoolexclusions@nas.org.uk

Independent Parental Special Education Advice http://www.ipsea.org.uk/

You should ask the governing board whether it has a clear process in place for considering reinstatement following an exclusion.

Things to consider

Do governors have an understanding of the exclusion process to enable a review within deadlines?

Would governors benefit from additional training, including on the Equality Act 2010?

Is there a clear and timely system in place to enable parents to make representations?

Are there up-to-date templates for notifying parents of the decision and explaining next steps?

Taking the decision

You must take the decision whether to exclude (you cannot delegate this).

Things to consider

Have I investigated specific incidents with all parties in a sensitive and fair way?

Did I consider factors that could have contributed to the pupil's behaviour (e.g. SEND or bereavement) and have I taken these factors sufficiently into account?

Is exclusion the most appropriate and reasonable sanction, and consistent with the school's behaviour policy?

Are all the exclusion reasons clearly recorded, including the impact on others? Are they robust?

Is relevant evidence properly recorded/retained/documented? (e.g. summaries of interviews, past behaviour, sanctions and support provided.)

You must inform parents of the exclusion.

Things to consider

Has the school spoken to the parents to ensure they fully understand the type/scale of the incident?

Have I provided sufficient details in the exclusion notice letter on the reasons for the exclusion?

Does the notice contain all the required information as set out in section 4 of the statutory exclusion guidance?

Have I informed parents whether their child will be able to sit any national curriculum test(s) or public examination(s) occurring during the exclusion?

When several fixed-period exclusions have been issued in a term, have I informed parents of their right of representation to the governing board?

Further sources of information

Letter templates might be available from the local authority.

If the exclusion is permanent or takes the pupil's total school days of exclusion over five in a term or prevents them from taking a public examination or national curriculum test, you must inform the **governing board and local authority of the duration of the exclusion, or that it is permanent, and the reasons for it.**

Things to consider

Have I informed the governing board about whether they must consider reinstatement and, if so, to what timescale?

Have I made clear to the governing board whether the need to consider reinstatement is dependent on receiving parental representations?

If a permanently excluded pupil lives in a different local authority area, has that authority been informed?

You should ask the chair of the governing board whether there are clear processes in place to comply with its legal duty to arrange suitable full-time educational provision for pupils of compulsory school age from the sixth consecutive school day of fixed-period exclusion.

Things to consider

Is there a process in place for the governing board to assure itself that the education provided is suitable and full-time?

Has the provision been quality assured and have previous placements been evaluated?

Is the education supervised? (Pupils doing unsupervised school work at home is not acceptable.)

Is there a process in place to monitor the pupil's attendance and behaviour at the provision?

Is the correct attendance code being used?

Further sources of information

Alternative provision guidance https://www.gov.uk/government/publications/alternative- provision

School attendance guidance https://www.gov.uk/government/publications/school- attendance

Governing board consideration of an exclusion decision

You should ask the chair of the governing board whether there are clear processes in place for considering exclusions.

Things to consider

Am I confident that the parents are aware of their right to a consideration by the governing board?

Has the governing board been appropriately involved?

Has the governing board taken steps to find a convenient date that the parent, the local authority representative (if relevant) and I can attend, within the legal time limits?

Where practicable, has the governing board given thought as to how to involve the pupil in the consideration process?

Have all the relevant documents been collected, anonymised if required, and provided to all parties?

Where applicable, the governing board **must** consider whether the pupil should be reinstated and inform parents of the outcome of its consideration.

Things to consider

Have I presented all of the details of the case and the full rationale for the exclusion?

Does the governing board have all of the relevant information that I have?

Independent review panel

The local authority or academy trust **must** arrange an independent review panel if requested by the parents within the time limit.

Things to consider

Do I need to make written representations and/or attend the meeting to make oral representations?

When applicable, the governing board **must** reconsider the exclusion within ten school days of being given notice of the independent review panel decision.

Things to consider

Is the governing board aware of any order made by the independent review panel following a direction (not a recommendation) to reconsider, and if this has been made, that unless within 10 school days of receiving notice of the panel's decision, the governing board decides to reinstate the pupil, the school will pay £4,000 to the local authority within 28 days?

The governing board **must** inform the head teacher, parents and local authority of its reconsideration decision.

Things to consider

If the pupil is reinstated, how should I ensure the pupil's effective reintegration?

If relevant, is the governing board aware that it must place a note on the pupil's record?

Post-exclusion action

When removing a pupil from the school roll, you **should** remind the governing board that they **must** ensure this is done under the circumstances prescribed by the Education (Pupil Registration) (England) Regulations 2006, as amended.

If applicable, you should check that the pupil's name has been removed from the school roll at the appropriate time.

Things to consider

Have I ensured that the common transfer file is transferred within 15 school days of the pupil ceasing to be registered at the school?

Further sources of information

Attendance Guidance and Education (Pupil Registration) (England) Regulations 2006 as amended
https://www.gov.uk/government/publications/school-attendance

School to School service: how to transfer information https://www.gov.uk/guidance/school-to-school-service-how-to-transfer-information

Special educational needs and disability code of practice: 0-25 years
https://www.gov.uk/government/uploads/system/uploads/attachment_data/file/398815/SEND_Code_of_Practice_January_2015.pdf

Children Missing Education statutory guidance https://www.gov.uk/government/publications/children-missing-educationl

Annex C – A guide for parents/carers

Parent/Carer Guide on Exclusion

Disclaimer

This non-statutory document is not replacing the statutory guidance on exclusion and is intended only to support parents' understanding of the exclusion process.

The exclusion legislation applies to maintained schools; pupil referral units (PRUs); and academies/free schools - other than 16-19 academies. It applies to all pupils at these schools, including those who are above or below compulsory school age, for example where a school also has a nursery or a sixth form. It does not apply to fee-paying independent schools, stand-alone nurseries, stand-alone sixth form colleges and other post-16 provision, such as Further Education colleges. These have their own exclusion arrangements.

If you are unsure in which category your child's school fits, you can find this information in Edubase:
http://www.education.gov.uk/edubase/about.xhtml

Glossary

The term **'must'** refers to what head teachers/governing boards/academy trusts/local authorities and parents are required to do by law. The term **'should'** refers to recommendations for good practice as mentioned in the exclusions guidance.

In this document and in the exclusion guidance, **'parents'** refers to parent(s)/legal guardian(s)/foster carer(s) of pupils under 18, as well as to pupils over 18, and the term **'governing board'** includes the governing body of a maintained school, the management committee of a PRU and the academy trust of an academy.

Fixed-period exclusion: when a pupil is barred from the school for a fixed amount of time (including exclusions during lunchtime).

Permanent exclusion: when a pupil is permanently barred from the school premises.

Alternative provision: This refers to the education arrangements made for excluded pupils to continue to have a suitable, full-time education whilst they are excluded from school or cannot attend school for another reason. In some circumstances, alternative provision can be used where a child has not been excluded, including alongside mainstream or special education, or for a placement to address poor behaviour.

Reasons for exclusion

For what reasons can a school exclude my child?

There is no list of set behaviours for which a pupil can and cannot be excluded, and the decision to exclude lies with the head teacher. Head teachers can only exclude a pupil for a disciplinary reason (e.g. because their behaviour violates the school's behaviour policy). They cannot, for example, exclude a pupil for academic performance/ability, or simply because they have additional needs or a disability that the school feels it is unable to meet. A head teacher can exclude for behaviour outside of school, or for repeatedly disobeying academic instructions.

Can the school send my child to be educated elsewhere?

Schools have the power to send a pupil to another education provider at a different location to improve their behaviour without the parents having to agree.

A school can also transfer a pupil to another school – a process called a 'managed move'

if they have the agreement of everyone involved, including the parents and the admission authority for the new school.

Schools cannot force a parent to remove their child permanently from the school or to keep their child out of school for any period of time without formally excluding. The threat of exclusion must never be used to influence parents to remove their child from the school.

Can a school ask me to collect my child/send my child home early without following the formal exclusions process?

'Informal' or 'unofficial' exclusions, such as sending pupils home 'to cool off', are not allowed, even if they are with the agreement of parents. Any exclusion of a pupil, even for short periods of time, must follow the formal process including being formally recorded (see below). Any fixed-period exclusion must have a stated end date.

Exclusion process

What happens when my child is excluded?

Please go to section 2 entitled 'What happens when your child is excluded' on the gov.uk website.
https://www.gov.uk/school-discipline-exclusions/exclusions

What are the legal obligations on a school when excluding a pupil?

When a head teacher excludes a pupil, they must without delay let parents know the type of exclusion and the reason(s) for it. They must also, without delay, provide parents with the following information in writing:

the reason(s) for the exclusion;

the length of the exclusion;

the parents' right to put forward their case about the exclusion to the governing board, how they should go about doing this and how the pupil can be involved; and

when relevant, what alternative provision will be provided from the sixth day of a fixed-period exclusion.

Is there a limit to the number of times my child can be excluded?

Yes. A pupil cannot be excluded for more than 45 school days in one school year. This means they cannot have one fixed-period exclusion of 46 school days or more; and also, they cannot have lots of shorter fixed-period exclusions that add up to more than 45 school days. This is true even if these exclusions have been given in different schools. Lunchtime exclusions - where pupils are excluded from school over the lunch period because this is when their behaviour is a problem - are counted as half a day.

Scrutiny of the exclusion

Can I question the decision to exclude my child?

Parents have the right to make their case about the exclusion of their child to the governing board. For fixed-period exclusions, unless the exclusion takes a pupil's total number of school days of exclusion past five in that term, the governing board must consider any case made by parents, but it cannot make the school reinstate the pupil and is not required to meet the parents.

For all permanent exclusions, the governing board must consider, within 15 school days of being told about the exclusion, whether the excluded pupil should be reinstated. This is the same for fixed-period exclusions where the pupil will miss more than 15 days in one term or will miss a public examination (e.g. a GCSE) or a national curriculum test (e.g. a key stage 2 test taken at the end of primary school). For a fixed-period exclusion that brings a pupil's total excluded days to more than five but under 15 the governing board must consider reinstatement within 50 school days if the parent asks it to do this.

If the governing board decides not to reinstate the pupil who has been permanently excluded, parents can request an independent review panel to review the governing board's decision.

Information on school discipline and exclusions issued by the Department for Education can be found here https://www.gov.uk/school-discipline-exclusions/exclusions.

What can I do if I feel my child is being discriminated against in the exclusion process, for example because he/she has a disability?

Schools have a duty under the Equality Act 2010 not to discriminate against pupils on the basis of protected characteristics, such as disability or race, including in all stages of the exclusion process.

Parents can raise this issue during the exclusion consideration meeting with the governing board.

If the governing board decides not to reinstate the pupil who has been permanently excluded, parents can request an independent review panel to review the governing board's decision. When making their request parents can ask for a Special Educational Needs (SEN) expert to attend the hearing to advise the panel on how SEN might be relevant to the exclusion. Parents can request this even if their child has not been officially recognised as having SEN.

If a parent believes that their child has been discriminated against in the exclusion process because of a disability, then they may also make a claim to the First-tier Tribunal (Special Educational Needs and Disability) within six months of the exclusion: www.tribunals.gov.uk/Tribunals/Firsttier/firsttier.htm. The Tribunal can consider claims about permanent and fixed-period exclusions. For permanent exclusions, this can be done instead of, or in addition to, an independent review panel.

If the parent believes that a permanent or fixed period exclusion occurred as a result of discrimination other than in relation to disability (e.g. in relation to race) they can make a claim to the County Court.

Where can I get independent advice on my options regarding the exclusion?

There are a number of organisations that provide free information, support and advice to parents on exclusion matters:

Coram Children's Legal Centre can be contacted on 0345 345 4345 or through http://www.childrenslegalcentre.com/index.php?page=education_legal_practice.

ACE education runs a limited advice line service on 0300 0115 142 on Monday to Wednesday from 10 am to 1 pm during term time. Information can be found on the website: http://www.ace-ed.org.uk/.

The National Autistic Society (Schools Exclusion Service (England) can be contacted on 0808 800 4002 or through: http://www.autism.org.uk/services/helplines/school-exclusions.aspx

Independent Parental Special Education Advice http://www.ipsea.org.uk/

You may also wish to access the following sources of advice from the Department for Education:

Departmental advice on setting the behaviour policy https://www.gov.uk/government/publications/behaviour-and-discipline-in-schools

The Department's guidance to schools on exclusion https://www.gov.uk/government/publications/school-exclusion.

'School discipline and exclusions' and 'Complaint about a school or childminder': https://www.gov.uk/school-discipline-exclusions/exclusions and https://www.gov.uk/complain-about-school.

Arrangements for my child after exclusion

Will my child still receive an education?

Schools should take reasonable steps to set work for pupils during the first five days of a fixed-period exclusion.

From the sixth day of an exclusion, suitable full-time education must be arranged for pupils of compulsory school age (primary and secondary school age), except for Year 11 pupils (final year of secondary school) whose final exams have passed. In the case of a fixed-period exclusion of more than five school days, it is the duty of the school to arrange this education, unless the school is a PRU (in which case the local authority should make arrangements). If a parent wishes to raise a concern about lack of, or the quality of, education arranged during a fixed-period exclusion (and their child is still of compulsory school age), they may follow the school's official complaints procedure.

In the case of a permanent exclusion, arranging suitable full-time education is the duty of the local authority for the area where the pupil lives. If a parent wishes to raise a concern about lack of, or the quality of, education following a permanent exclusion (and their child is still of compulsory school age), parents should complain to the local authority where they live. If parents are unsure about which local authority they need to speak to, they should ask the school for advice.

Does my child still have a right to attend their exams or national curriculum tests when excluded?

This is a decision for the school. Neither the school nor the local authority is legally required to arrange for an excluded pupil to take a public examination or national curriculum test that occurs during the exclusion, although some may choose to arrange for this, either on school premises or elsewhere. Where a parent has concerns about their child missing a public examination or national curriculum test, they should raise these with the school.

What are my duties as a parent when my child has been excluded?

For the first five school days of any exclusion, parents must ensure that their child of compulsory school age is not in a public place during school hours without very good reason. Parents must also ensure that their child attends any new full-time education provided from the sixth day of exclusion (unless they have arranged suitable alternative education themselves).

Footnotes

[1] Education (Provision of Full-Time Education for Excluded Pupils) (England) (Amendment) Regulations 2014, amending the Education (Provision of Full-Time Education for Excluded Pupils) (England) Regulations 2007.

[2] Section 51A Education Act 2002 and regulations made under that section.

[3] In a maintained school, 'head teacher' includes an acting head teacher by virtue of section 579(1) of the Education Act 1996. An acting head teacher is someone appointed to carry out the functions of the head teacher in the head teacher's absence or pending the appointment of a head teacher. This will not necessarily be the deputy head teacher: it will depend who is appointed to the role of acting head teacher. In an academy, 'principal' includes acting principal by virtue of regulation 21 of the School Discipline (Pupil Exclusions and Reviews) (England) Regulations 2012.

[4] Non-statutory advice from the Department for Education is available to help schools to understand how the Equality Act affects them and how to fulfil their duties under the Act and can be downloaded at the following link: https://www.gov.uk/government/publications/equality-act-2010-advice-for-schools.

[5] The SEND code of practice can be found here: https://www.gov.uk/government/publications/send-code- of-practice-0-to-25.

[6] Section 29A of the Education Act 2002. The legal requirements and statutory guidance relating to this power are set out in guidance on alternative provision: https://www.gov.uk/government/publications/alternative-provision.

[7] Non-statutory guidance for head teachers of maintained schools on the place of multi-agency assessments in a school's behaviour policy is provided by *Behaviour and Discipline in Schools – A Guide for Head teachers and School Staff* (2015) https://www.gov.uk/government/publications/behaviour-and- discipline-in-schools.

[8] As defined in section 22 of the Children Act 1989.

[9] References to pupils with EHC plans include pupils with statements of SEN whilst they remain.

[10] Section 51A Education Act 2002 and regulations made under that section.

[11] Section 572 Education Act 1996

[12] Sections 103 to 105 Education and Inspections Act 2006 and regulations made under these sections.

[13] Section 51A Education Act 2002 and regulations made under that section.

[14] As set out in the Education (Information About Individual Pupils) (England) Regulations 2013.

[15] Section 100 of the Education and Inspections Act 2006, section 19 of the Education Act 1996 and regulations made under those sections.

[16] The education arranged must be full-time or as close to full-time as in the child's best interests because of their health needs.

[17] Section 44 of the Children and Families Act 2014 provides for reviews and reassessments, with further detail in Part 2 of the Special Educational Needs and 'Disability Regulations 2014.

[18] Section 51A Education Act 2002 and regulations made under that section, as well as the School Governance (Roles, Procedures and Allowances) (England) Regulations 2013.

[19] A governing board is no longer prevented from meeting within the five school days after an exclusion.

[20] Where the chair is unable to make this consideration, then the vice-chair may do so instead.

[21] Parents may request that the local authority and/or the home local authority attend a meeting of an academy's governing board as an observer; that representative may only make representations with the governing board's consent.

[22] Section 51A Education Act 2002 and regulations made under that section.

[23] Section 51A Education Act 2002 and regulations made under that section.

[24] Regulations 8(1)(m), 8(3)(e) and 8(4)(d) of the Education (Pupil Registration) (England) Regulations 2006, as amended, set out the circumstances in which a permanently excluded pupil must be removed from the register. Regulation 12(7) of the Education (Pupil Registration) (England) Regulations 2006 as inserted by Regulation 5 of the Education (Pupil Registration) (England) (Amendment) Regulations 2016 sets out the information that must be submitted to the local authority.

[25] Departmental advice on attendance codes can be found at the following link: https://www.gov.uk/government/publications/school-attendance.

[25] Departmental advice on attendance codes can be found at the following link:

https://www.gov.uk/government/publications/school-attendance.

[26] Section 51A Education Act 2002 and regulations made under this section.

[27] The First-tier Tribunal (Special Educational Needs and Disability) and County Court have the jurisdiction to hear claims of discrimination under the Equality Act 2010 which relate to exclusions.

[28] In such circumstances, the Tribunal or Court may decide to delay its consideration until after the independent review panel process has been completed.

[29] When arranging a venue for the review, the local authority/academy trust must comply with its duties under the Equality Act 2010 and consider what reasonable adjustments should be made to support the attendance and contribution of parties at the review (for example where a parent or pupil has a disability in relation to mobility or communication that impacts upon his/her ability to attend the meeting or to make representations).

[30] Section 51A Education Act 2002 and regulations made under that section.

[31] Head teachers/principals/teachers in charge of a PRU and governors/management committee members of maintained schools, PRUs and Academies are eligible to be members of independent review panels considering an exclusion from any type of school covered by this guidance.

[32] Section 51A Education Act 2002 and regulations made under this section.

[33] Section 51A Education Act 2002 and regulations made under this section.

[34] Section 51A Education Act 2002 and regulations made under this section.

[35] Section 51A Education Act 2002 and regulations made under this section.

[36] Section 51A Education Act 2002 and regulations made under this section.

[37] Section 51A Education Act 2002 and regulations made under this section. The requirements for the transfer of funding following an exclusion from a maintained school or PRU are set out in The Education (Amount to Follow Permanently Excluded Pupil) Regulations 1999. Academy funding agreements may require an academy to enter into a similar agreement with the local authority.

[38] This does not include circumstances where a school or academy has voluntarily entered into a separate legally binding agreement with the local authority.

[39] At a maintained school or PRU, the head teacher must determine the behaviour policy in accordance with principles set out by the governing board. An academy trust must have a behaviour policy, but it is up to the academy trust to decide who is responsible for drawing up the policy.

Bibliography

Always Someone Else's Problem, Children's Commissioner

https://www.childrenscommissioner.gov.uk/wp-content/uploads/2017/07/Always_Someone_Elses_Problem.pdf

They Never Give Up on You, Children's Commissioner

https://www.childrenscommissioner.gov.uk/wp-content/uploads/2017/07/They-never-give-up-on-you-final-report.pdf

They Go the Extra Mile, Children's Commissioner

https://www.childrenscommissioner.gov.uk/wp-content/uploads/2017/07/They_Go_The_Extra_Mile-.pdf

Exclusions from Maintained Schools, Academies and Pupil Referral Units in England: Statutory guidance for those with legal responsibilities in relation to exclusion, DfE

https://assets.publishing.service.gov.uk/government/uploads/system/uploads/attachment_data/file/641418/20170831_Exclusion_Stat_guidance_Web_version.pdf

Exploring School Exclusion Statistics, DfE

https://department-for-education.shinyapps.io/exclusion-statistics/

School Complaints Procedures, DfE

https://www.gov.uk/government/publications/school-complaints-procedures/best-practice-advice-for-school-complaints-procedures-2019

Harris, N. & Eden, K. (2000) *Challenges to School Exclusion.* (Routledge)

Ward, J. (2019) *On the Fringes.* (Crown House)

Index

Absence, 24, 38, 39, 52, 54, 76, 94, 119, 120, 124, 138, 167, 182, 183, 203
Alternatives, 8, 9, 12, 41, 69, 138, 189, 195, 198
Alternative Provision, 8, 9, 58, 59, 119
Appeals, 86, 105
Attendance, 31, 38, 51, 52, 82, 89, 94, 113, 118, 119, 120, 122, 168, 173, 179, 184, 187, 189, 195, 197, 204
Behaviour Policy, 19, 21, 25, 27, 31, 32, 34, 44, 45, 47, 76, 85, 86, 99, 103, 138, 144, 159, 161, 192, 194, 198, 201, 203, 204
Complaints, 81, 84, 85, 114, 139, 205
Discrimination, 96
Duty of Care, 66
Early Intervention, 47, 48, 161
EHC Plan, 9, 15, 44, 69, 71, 95, 136, 139
Equalities Act, 96, 153
Exams, 106, 121, 139
Fines, 38, 72, 81, 119
Fixed Term Exclusion, 9, 12, 41
Free School Meals, 14, 15, 88, 162
Full-time Education, 50
Governors, 5, 71, 84, 99, 100, 106, 109, 110, 121, 137, 139, 175
Headteacher, 24, 27, 65, 84, 106, 110, 136, 139
Internal, 60
Letter, 19, 43, 45, 67, 76, 79, 81, 84, 86, 102, 103, 117, 119, 120, 122, 140, 142, 143, 144, 149, 150, 164, 170, 171, 183, 187, 194
Managed Moves, 53, 54

Multi-agency Assessment, 49, 159, 162, 192
OFSTED, 7, 58, 84, 91, 129, 130
Parental Responsibility, 117
Part-time Timetable, 10, 32, 38, 50, 51, 52, 56, 58, 137, 143, 154
Pastoral Support Plan, 10, 61
Permanent Exclusion, 13, 14, 16, 17, 37, 38, 40, 42, 43, 44, 53, 55, 56, 67, 71, 79, 95, 106, 110, 111, 116, 117, 124, 128, 133, 134, 136, 138, 140, 142, 149, 151, 159, 160, 163, 165, 170, 173, 182, 187, 193, 198, 202
Persistent Disruption, 13, 14, 25, 29, 48, 52
Physical Assault, 13, 14
Proof, 64, 160, 169, 181
Public Spaces, 122
Pupil Referral Units, 16, 56, 205
Reintegration, 73, 140, 141
SAR, 81, 82, 83
SENCO/SENDCO, 5, 9, 24, 27, 37, 48, 131, 136, 139, 142, 143
Special Educational Needs/SEN, 5, 9, 12, 14, 15, 27, 30, 32, 48, 49, 53, 60, 66, 73, 76, 81, 87, 90, 91, 92, 94, 97, 98, 99, 100, 101, 102, 103, 106, 113, 116, 129, 133, 144, 145, 153, 155, 157, 159, 161, 162, 179, 180, 183, 184, 192, 193, 200, 203
Statements, 78, 193
Transfer, 62
Verbal Assault, 14
Vulnerable Groups, 87

Printed in Great Britain
by Amazon